Typography: **Macro- and Microaesthetics**

In order to know an object, I must know not its external but all its internal qualities.

Ludwig Wittgenstein, 1918

Willi Kunz

Typography: Macro- and Microaesthetics

Niggli

Second printing, 2000
Revised, expanded edition.

Copyright © 1998 by
Verlag Niggli AG
Sulgen | Zürich

Printed in Switzerland
ISBN 3-7212-0348-8

Library of Congress
Catalog Card Number
98-91729

Published by
Verlag Niggli AG
Steinackerstrasse 8
8583 Sulgen
Switzerland

English language edition
available from

Willi Kunz Books
2112 Broadway
New York, NY 10023
212 799 4300
212 877 7024 fax
wkany@aol.com

Typography is the art of designing letters and composing text so that they may be read easily, efficiently, enjoyably. Certain fundamental principles underlie all good typography – be it in newspapers, magazines or books; on posters, packaging or computer screens. First established with Gutenberg's moveable type, then developed by Modernism's visual revolutions, these same principles will still be valid in the dawning age of electronic media: hypertext, Internet – whatever fora the future may bring.

This book sets out the enduring principles of typography, explains how to apply them, and illustrates their power and versatility with examples drawn from my twenty-five years of professional experience. By demonstrating how theory actually is put into practice, Typography: Macro and Microaesthetics provides artistic and technical instruction for typographic designers, architects, and professionals in allied creative fields. In addition, by analyzing the role graphic design plays in today's media-dominated culture, it facilitates a more critical appreciation not only of the mediated foreground, but also of the unscripted background and of the various relationships between one and the other.

Most books on typography only show the end product; they tell nothing about either the process of designing or the principles of design. Design annuals and glossy magazines are no better: the one is but vanity portfolio; the other but shootings of stars and trends fated to fade out by the next issue. In circular fashion, students imitate stars, designers follow trends, clients survey markets, and the public drowns in a great graphic "sea" without ever learning how to look for and at good typography. This book provides sextant and compass for charting a new course in today's inundation of information.

The Information Age has arrived. And though with it the death of print media has – yet again – been predicted, paper proliferates. In the 1930s and 1950s it was said, "This will kill that;" but first radio and then television did not kill newspapers, magazines, books. Nor in the 1980s did the wired office create the paperless office. To the contrary, at home, at work, commuting in between, we all are expected to process more and more information printed on paper. Consequently, we not only have less and less time to peruse each item; also, concomitantly, we are less and less willing to labor over material that's poorly presented. Small wonder so much printed matter is discarded – the unread flotsam and jetsam of our civilization.

If printed paper is the problem, then are electronic media the solution? Yes and no. Books and computers each serve different purposes, one better than the other. Computers are the superior medium for searching out small pieces of information in sources which are very large, constantly changing, or highly individual: data bases, market quotes, and "bulletin boards," for example. They also have the added advantage that discards become ether, not landfill. Computers are the inferior medium, however, for reading long, involved text;

rather than studying a screen for hours on end, most people will print out and work on hard copy: they will, in effect, "publish" a page, a chapter, an individually edited book.

Books are a familiar format. They're simple to use and easy to transport; they work without complicated software or costly hardware. Books supplement the literary pleasures of a text with sensual satisfactions – with the visual, tactile and aesthetic qualities of paper, typography, printing and binding. Books, moreover, have an "aura;" on a shelf in a library they impart a sense of intellectual community and historic continuity that CD's in a rack just don't possess; can't finesse.

While books will always be the ultimate exemplars of print typography, electronic media also display words and images whose design must be coherent and convincing to the passive viewer. Interactive media require in addition that design be comprehensible and convenient for the active user. Hypertext is the extreme case in which the design of the original must be so comprehensively structured that it can accommodate any and all deconstructions, reassemblies, and idiosyncrasies of innumerable individual "authors." Ironically, that structure can only come from those fundamental principles of typography first formulated in the Gutenberg Bible of 1455.

Today, it is important to make a distinction between fundamental visual principles and traditional technical standards. Many of the latter arose when design and typesetting were separate professions and coordination between them required exact specification of type face and size, line length, etc. Inevitably, those specifications became not only means of communication but also ends in themselves – impersonal, technical criteria according to which typography could be designed and evaluated.

The facility of computer graphics software has both folded the role of typesetter into that of designer and eliminated the need for traditional technical standards. Typography is now created according to more personal, visual criteria. Criteria, nevertheless, remain crucial; without them – without fundamental principles – typography could no more communicate visually than could language without grammar and vocabulary communicate verbally. Typography: Macro- and Microaesthetics elaborates those principles. Specifically, the book first analyzes space, structure, sequence, contrast, form and counterform; it then demonstrates how these elements can be synthesized to create a body of work in print and electronic media.

My approach to typography is not the only one. But an understanding of the principles underlying it are necessary both to create and appreciate alternative approaches, other styles. Without those principles, one can do nothing of consequence; with them, one can do whatever he/she will. The fundamental principles of typography are simple, powerful means to various, sophisticated ends.

I would like to thank all whose collaboration has been essential in creating the first edition of Typography: Macro- and Microaesthetics and the publisher, Verlag Niggli AG, for their commitment to produce again a high-quality book. Also, I am deeply grateful to the designers, educators and students who made this new edition of Typography: Macro- and Microaesthetics possible so soon.

Introduction

Whenever we speak or write, we communicate. Language, whether spoken or written, is part of what makes us unique as humans. Spoken language is ephemeral and intangible, it disappears as soon as it is uttered. When written, language is captured in a visual and spatial form, permanent and concrete. As the art of visual language, typography is inherently communicative.

Like language, typography is both functional and expressive, serving purposes of utility and beauty. The function of typography is to communicate a message so that it effectively conveys both its intellectual meaning and its emotional feeling. This is a cognitive task, making use of letters and words which can be recognized and comprehended by the reader. At the heart of good typographic design is a critical interpretation of the meaning of the message: the more astute the interpretation, the more effective the design.

If function is important to the intellect, then form is important to the emotions. Form is the aesthetic component of design; it is what attracts attention, invites participation, and offers enjoyment. Our day-to-day life is enriched or degraded by the aesthetic qualities of our environment. A neglected building is not only unattractive to look at, but also depressing, thus affecting us psychologically. Likewise, poorly designed visual communication assaults our sensibilities, creating a kind of visual pollution.

Typographic form and message content are inextricably linked. Even the simplest design not only objectively conveys information but also gives subjective cues for the interpretation of this content. Typography seeks to integrate and balance form and function, recognizing the importance of each. Function without form is dull; form without function or purpose lacks substance and meaning.

Perhaps the most difficult task faced by the typographic designer is to master this balance. An interesting visual effect may enhance a message, but it can also overwhelm it. When form dominates content, form in fact becomes the message and the content is weakened, even lost. Such design may initially look exciting, but it lacks depth, honesty, and conviction. On the other hand, if form were inconsequential, typography would become rote and dull. A message would be communicated on a cognitive level, but the artistic purpose of typography – to inspire and delight – would have vanished.

The argument that visually challenging typography will entice a reader to decipher a message is invalid. Complexity is an obstacle, not an invitation. As more and more information becomes available, less and less time is spent consuming each piece. Attention spans shorten, powers of concentration decrease – and an impenetrable message will be passed over in favor of something more accessible. Typography must not only allow people to read and comprehend information, but make it both easy and pleasurable to do so. Given the amount of information we are confronted with each day, this consideration is vital.

It is less difficult to create an exclusively aesthetic solution than to create a solution that communicates effectively while remaining visually appealing. Designers must be diligent in ensuring that the aesthetics of a design do not overwhelm its content. When in doubt, it is more appropriate to adhere to the basic typographic principles that stress function than to resort to unbridled self-expression. And in the visually chaotic environment in which we find ourselves today, simple solutions often look fresh and unexpected.

A design that pleases the eye is always more effective than one that does not. What pleases, however, is a contentious point. The one certainty is that no two people appreciate – or create – design in exactly the same way. Where one person might intellectually analyze a visual composition, another might intuitively sense the harmony of a design. Sensibilities differ. Such differences produce variety. They also produce disagreement about which designs are good, and why.

Lacking analytical, consensual terms, decisions become based on vague notions, "gut" reactions, and unproven authority, prejudicing discourse among designers and their clients. The inevitable results are not only less than optimal but – wanting constructive, critical tools – beyond repair.

The primary constructive tools for typographic design are a knowledge of communications theory, a good grasp of typographic principles, knowledge of the intended audience, and a clear focus on the goals of the communication, rather than on nebulous aesthetic ambitions. These principles are the general foundation on which specific designs can be built and evaluated; they focus the design process and making it more manageable. Weaknesses in a design can be more productively discussed when measured against specific semantic, syntactic, and pragmatic criteria.

A focus on the objective goals and concerns of the design process is necessary for any design, yet in itself it does not guarantee a good solution. Good typographic design must also create a perceptual, subjective effect: in other words, aesthetic pleasure.

Aesthetics are more difficult to judge than the clarity of a message because aesthetic taste is more personal and culturally specific. Deciding on the visual style or treatment that will best convey the message is more problematic than choosing the words and composing the sentences that communicate the objective and subjective content. There are no visual dictionaries or grammar books to define the subtleties and exactitudes of meaning of any particular visual representation. Aesthetics must be adapted to the environment in which the communication takes place. Fitting the aesthetics to their context is a complex process and must take into account not only the historical moment and cultural context, but also the graphic medium and the socioeconomic status and level of education of the intended audience.

Many designers make the relationship of visual elements (syntax) their primary concern. In practice, the stress on visual syntax often detracts from meaning (semantics) and each element's effect and affect on the reader (pragmatics). A design may be exciting to the designer, but fail to resonate with its audience. In the initial stage of a design, visual syntax should not be the main concern, because a message is never communicated on a purely syntactical level. It is more important to find the forms of expression appropriate for the particular audience. In many instances, designers face the choice between satisfying their own aesthetic sensibilities and ambitions and creating a design for an audience with very different tastes and needs. To find and work with an aesthetic that supports communication and stimulates the reader, designers must constantly expand and refine their intellectual capacity and visual sensitivity.

The rapid introduction of new technology into the practice of typographic design has caused confusion about its role in the design process. The computer has replaced the automobile as the latest fetish of our techno-consumer society. Computer power, programs, and capabilities are discussed endlessly, with no less ignorance than reverence. Whatever has been generated digitally is deemed state-of-the-art and good; everything else is obsolete and bad. Rarely do such discussions consider the quality of the actual work produced on – not by – computers. Increasingly, it is forgotten that it is the designer's intelligence, not the software, which makes the difference between mediocre and outstanding design.

The explosion of desktop publishing and the proliferation of computers do not, themselves, weaken the designer's importance. Rather, the triumph of the computer only intensifies the need for intelligent, aesthetically pleasing design. The postindustrial information age, if it means nothing else, means more messages: messages that must be sorted, sifted, and represented in ways that people understand, enjoy, and most importantly, can use. As we become inundated with information, thoughtful, perceptive design will become a more important mark of distinction, a competitive edge.

The information age also presents new challenges to the designer: electronic media, virtual reality, interactive TV, and other modes of expression which have yet to be developed present largely unexplored territory for intelligent design. The skills already possessed by designers – organizing and visually displaying information, managing the interplay between the verbal and the visual – continue to be essential in new media. This is not to say that designers need not learn new skills, it emphasizes that their old skills will not become obsolete. The semantic, syntactic, and pragmatic principles of typographic design provide a firm basis from which to approach old challenges as well as new. The flexibility required to produce vital, creative work can come only from a deep rooting in these principles.

How do principles apply in a world that is drowning in information and reeling with distraction? Do principles inhibit creativity and individual development when typography is about exploring new directions? Principles are important in everything we do, in typography as well as in life. Principles are not ends in themselves, rather they are points of orientation highly open to interpretation; they constitute a road map which may look very clear but does not convey a picture of the final destination. Even when principles are strictly applied, the end result is always surprising.

Typography today is based on the same principles as it was centuries ago. And it must be so, as long as letters, words, and sentences communicate. We understand a message, or we don't. This does not mean that the design of visual communication should do no more than simply transmit information. A design should also enlighten the reader and further the continuity and history of typography. The best typography communicates the conviction that it has resolved a design problem in a way both central to that problem and at the outer limits of its own possibilities.

In typography, developments that last are not revolutionary; what is new and hot does not suddenly, completely replace what is old and cold. Rather, the significant new is evolutionary; it develops out of past traditions, while responding to present circumstances. Its persistence depends on its contribution to the continuum of typographic form and sensibilities.

Today, I sense an anxious anticipation among designers. Is this millennial fear? Is it professional uncertainty about the state and fate of design? Is it the rapid pace of technological change? Information anxiety?

For millennia, visual communication was a transaction of information within relatively small groups of people. With the invention of letterpress printing in the 15th century, the world entered a second phase of mass-produced and widely distributed information. The power of mass communication, however, was limited to those who had access to the specialist with printing equipment. With the introduction of personal computers, graphics software, and electronic media in the early 1980s, communications entered a third phase in which virtually everyone can send and receive messages. The result is a democratization of information with unpredictable consequences.

Other social pressures have caused uncertainty. Environmental concerns raise serious questions about the future of traditional print media. The nature of reading and attention are changing, too. Over the World Wide Web, information can be exchanged instantly around the world. The media increasingly presume that their audience processes information not by active reading and reflection but by passive looking and listening. Electronic media such as television and video promote info-nuggets, palatable and easily digested. Designers can adapt to the complexities and frustrations of working in today's cultural climate – but only if they learn to think flexibly: to abstract essentials from the information available, integrate it with their own methodologies, and create not according to style but principles.

Design is not a paint-by-numbers discipline – there are no prescribed solutions to the unimaginable diversity of communication problems. Instead, typographic designers rely on a process which enables them to assess each situation and respond with an appropriate solution based on their knowledge of typographic principles, visual sensitivity, and personal vision. It is this foundation that gives designers the flexibility and intelligence needed to meet the challenges of a fast-moving world, with its new contexts, media, and modes of communication. It makes typography exciting and pleasurable, an endeavor whose challenge can span a lifetime of work.

1

Elements of typography

Typography comprises a limited set of basic elements: letters, numbers, and punctuation marks.

Despite continuous changes in aesthetic preference, design theory, and reproduction methods, the basic forms of these elements have remained constant for the past 2000 years.

Alphabets derived from the original Latin are – and are likely always to be – indispensable to life in the western world. To conceive our culture and our environment without them is virtually impossible. No other system of visual communication has proven itself so powerful and versatile, yet so precise and concise in its transcription of facts, thoughts and feelings.

A B C   a b c

D E F G H   d e f g h

I J K L M   i j k l m

N O P Q R   n o p q r

S T U V W   s t u v w

X Y Z   x y z

Letters, numbers, punctuation marks

The basic elements of typography are upper case letters, lower case letters, numbers, and punctuation marks. Letters evolved from prehistoric pictographs and ideographs to become the sophisticated signs of the Latin alphabet – the most widely used system of writing in the world today.

Although over the centuries variations have been made in details, the essential structure of letters and numbers has undergone no significant change. Whether carved in stone, written on paper, printed in books, or pixelated on computers, letters have always used the same basic structure the Romans used.

Perhaps the most notable modification in the structure of letters occurred in the fourth century, when minuscules (lower case letters) were distinguished from majuscules (upper case letters). While the structure of twelve minuscules remained close to their corresponding majuscules, fourteen became sharply differentiated between upper- and lower case.

Another notable innovation was the appearance of a sans serif face in the early nineteenth century. Although little noticed until the late 1800s, today sans serif is widely recognized as embodying a radical sensibility which has had a profound impact on modern typography.

0123456789

,;:.!?¡¿

_ — —— ~

'' '' ,, '' '' '' ⟨⟩ ⟪⟫ ( ) [ ]

& / * †

*Monotype® Bembo.
The original version was
created by Francesco
Griffo da Bologna, Italy, in
the late 15th century.*

A a	C c
B b	I i
D d	K k
E e	O o
F f	P p
G g	S s
H h	U u
J j	V v
L l	W w
M m	Y y
N n	X x
Q q	Z z
R r	
T t	

Since the 1980s, computer graphics programs have provided
designers with access to virtually every version of the
Latin alphabet – access formerly restricted to printers and
typesetters. Though the selection of type styles is now
immense, the basic elements remain the same.

This limited set of basic elements – letters, numbers, and
punctuation marks – make typography an especially
challenging field of design. The contemporary designer
must constantly search for creative solutions to the
problem of communicating facts, thoughts, and feelings,
with just these few fecund elements.

*The structure of upper
case letters has changed
only minimally over the
course of centuries.
Lower case letters have
changed in varying
degrees. Some forms are
still closely related to
their upper case counter-
parts, others differ con-
siderably in their structure.*

abc　　　　A B C

defgh　　　D E F G H

ijklm　　　I J K L M

nopqr　　　N O P Q R

stuvw　　　S T U V W

xyz　　　　X Y Z

The diversity of human language, together with the need
for typography to express subtle inflections and convey
the structure of information, calls for a variety of additional letters and special signs.

Italics, termed oblique in sans serif type, are mainly used
to differentiate from roman type. Unobtrusive yet distinct,
italics are indispensable for emphasis. A true italic
typeface is vital: simulating an italic on the computer by
slanting a roman face produces letterforms with strangely
distorted proportions.

Small caps, slightly letterspaced for a more refined appearance, are primarily used for subtitles, acronyms, abbreviations and emphasis. They are designed to correspond
to the x-height and weight of lower case letters. Genuine
small caps are normally available only in expert fonts.

Reducing upper case letters to the height of lower
case produces small caps that are visually too light to be
compatible with text.

Old-style figures, also called text figures, are designed to
match the size of lower case letters. They blend more
smoothly with text, and are desirable for typefaces with a
small x-height. Old-style figures are common in serif
typefaces, but are generally available only in expert fonts.

0123456789

Bembo
Old-style figures.

*Each type font includes
a number of special
signs. The series of signs
below is available in
all fonts.*

Acute accent	ÁÉÍÓÚ	áéíóú
Grave accent	ÀÈÌÒÙ	àèìòù
Circumflex	ÂÊÎÔÛ	âêîôû
Umlaut	ÄÖÜ	äöü
Diaeresis	ËÏ	ëï
Tilde	ÃÑÕ	ãñõ
Ring accent	Å	å
Cedilla	Ç	ç
Slashed O	Ø	ø
Ligatures	Æ Œ	æ œ fi fl ß

at	@
Copyright	©
Registered	®
Trademark	TM
Degree	°
Space	#
Brace	{}
Paragraph	¶
Section	§
Dollar	$
Pound	£
Yen	¥
Euro	€

Accent marks, foreign punctuation marks, and other signs
   are essential for multilingual typography. On the computer,
   these symbols are inserted into the text through an
   often tedious process of single or multiple-step keyboard
   commands.
Ligatures combine two or three letters into a single character.
   They are available only in expert fonts, and are crucial
   for the refined setting of serif type. The ligatures fi and fl
   are, because of their frequency, the most important. Letterspaced text precludes the use of ligatures.

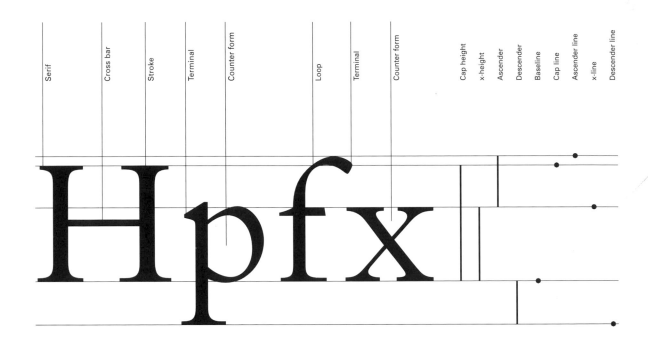

Serif | Cross bar | Stroke | Terminal | Counter form | Loop | Terminal | Counter form | Cap height | x-height | Ascender | Descender | Baseline | Cap line | Ascender line | x-line | Descender line

Variation of serifs:
bracketed serif
hairline serif
slab serif.

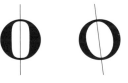

Variation of curve axis:
vertical
oblique.

The parts of letters

The terms used to designate the parts of letters originated
in metal typesetting. This terminology was indispensable
for collaboration between the typographic designer
and the typesetter, when their professions were distinct.
Although the computer has combined design and typesetting
into a single activity, the terminology remains essential
for comparing and evaluating individual typefaces, and for
specifying, measuring, and positioning type.

Set width

Character width

Mig

*Univers 55 with normal
set width.*

*Bodoni with normal
set width.*

*Bodoni with increased
set width.*

Character width and set width

In typographic design, it is important to distinguish between
the character width and the set width. The character
width is the effective visual width of an individual letter.
The set width, by contrast, includes the variable space
to the left and right of each letter. The set width is crucial
because it influences type legibility and text length.
Even small changes in set width can cause considerable
differences in the final length of the text.

On the computer, the set width is controlled by tracking.
Reducing the space between letters to less than the standard set width is not recommended for any text,
because excessively close letters will appear too tight
and create a spotty composition.

Renaissance-Antiqua
Bembo

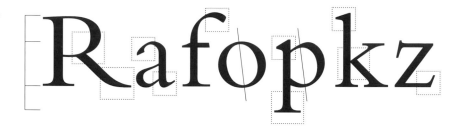

The uniqueness of each typeface is found in its microaesthetic details. Selection of a typeface is most strongly influenced by these details, which distinguish one typeface from another.

Baroque-Antiqua
Baskerville

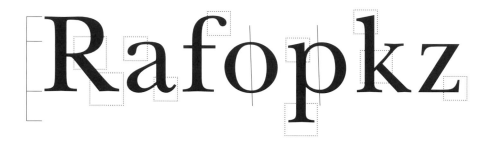

Neoclassical Antiqua
Bodoni

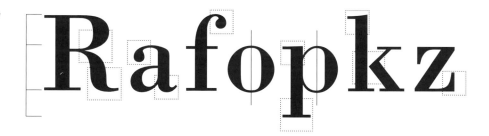

Variation of style

Our visual environment would be unbearably dull if a single typeface were applied universally. Individual typefaces, with their different styles and particular idiosyncrasies, all contribute to the visual expressiveness of typography. Only very few of the countless "new" typefaces produced and marketed every year serve a real need and promise to stand the test of time. Invariably they look dated after a few uses, and are soon superseded by a new crop.

Designers, in their quest for originality, often become preoccupied, even obsessed, with typefaces, with the unfortunate result that typefaces are used to mask weak ideas or are degraded into meaningless decoration. Typically, however, a general audience is more interested in content than in the typeface used. If the goal of typographic design is to communicate information, the audience is best served by a simple, classical typeface.

Technological advances and changes in taste will undoubtedly influence letterform design in the future. However, true developments are more than microaesthetic changes in existing styles. Mere embellishments on basic letterforms do not constitute new design, and actually work against the precepts of typography to communicate information clearly.

Most of the typefaces in use at present were created for printing on paper. On the screen or through electronic transmittal, most typefaces lose their refinements of detail and bear no resemblance to the original. Electronic media require new typefaces developed with their specific technical conditions in mind.

Slab serif
Rockwell

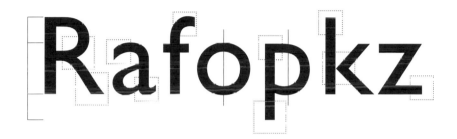

Sans serif
GIll

Sans serif
Meta

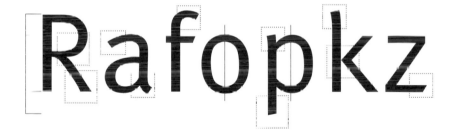

Characteristics of typefaces classified by five categories of styles. The date indicates when the typeface was first produced for metal or computer composition.	Renaissance-Antiqua	Baroque-Antiqua	Neoclassical Antiqua	Slab serif	Sans serif
	Strong modulation of curves	Moderate modulation of curves	Strong modulation of curves	Subtle modulation of curves	Subtle modulation of curves
	Bracketed serifs	Bracketed serifs	Straight hairline serifs	Bold straight or bracketed serifs	Vertical curve axis
	Oblique ascender terminals	Oblique ascender terminals	Horizontal ascender terminals	Horizontal ascender terminals	
	Oblique curve axis	Oblique curve axis	Vertical curve axis	Vertical curve axis	Akzidenz Grotesk, 1896
The subtle details of the original design are often lost when a typeface is re-issued in digital form. In selecting a typeface, it is best to choose the version of the date closest to the original design.					Franklin Gothic, 1903
	Caslon, 1916	Baskerville, 1923	Century, 1894	Memphis, 1929	Monotype Grotesk, 1926
	Goudy, 1916	Fournier, 1925	Walbaum, 1918	Beton, 1930	Gill Sans, 1927
	Janson, 1919	Bell, 1931	Bodoni, 1921	Rockwell, 1934	Futura, 1927
	Garamond, 1922		Centennial, 1986	Courier, 1945	Helvetica, 1957
	Bembo, 1929			Serifa, 1969	Univers, 1957
	Times, 1931				Syntax, 1968
	Van Dijck, 1935				Frutiger, 1976
	Sabon, 1965				Bell Centennial, 1978
					Formata, 1984
					Meta, 1991

A case for Univers

In connection with my work, I am often asked why I prefer Univers not only to serif typefaces but also to other sans serifs such as Futura, Gill, or Helvetica.

My own preference for Univers begins – but does not end – with its still-contemporary form and its comprehensive series of fonts. In the early 20th century, the vehement and animated debate between proponents and opponents of the new sans serif type required typographers to take a stand for one side or the other. Today, the issue of serifs versus sans serif is no longer of aesthetic relevance or ideological interest: the decision to use one face or the other is better made on the basis of functionality and appropriateness.

Traditionalists argue that serif type is more readable than sans serif. While this may be so with lengthy text, readability is in most cases less a function of the presence of serifs in the typeface than of other factors: namely type size, weight, and slant; line length and interline space; paper, printing, and reading conditions. In fact, the most important determinant of legibility (clarity and efficiency in reading) and readability (pleasure and interest in reading) is not the particular typeface but the arrangement and structure of information.

Throughout my professional career, I have worked with many sans serif typefaces; among them all I have found Univers uniquely versatile. Univers has neither the rigid forms of Helvetica nor the geometric constructions of Futura; unlike Gill and many other sans serif faces it comprises a series complete in terms of weights as well as widths. Univers, moreover, is quietly refined in its visual details; nothing extraneous detracts from the essential form of individual letters. The upper case letters, which are only slightly heavier than lower "read" distinctly but unobtrusively in lengthy texts.

Univers was created in the early 1950s by Adrian Frutiger, a Swiss type designer with a profound knowledge of the history of type and print technology. The first typeface ever conceived as a complete series, Univers consists of 21 fonts, with Univers 55 serving as the primary font from which the other 20 were developed. Univers 55 manifests all the characteristics of a good text typeface. Its large x-height with short ascenders and descenders makes the font compact yet readable in small point sizes.

Univers was designed as a matrix with 55 at the center: to the left are expanded fonts, to the right condensed; above light, below bold. Each font is identified by a two-digit number. The first digit indicates weight, the second slant; roman is indicated by odd numbers, italics by even. Inherent in this matrix of 21 fonts are countless possibilities for visual contrast in typographic design.

Since the introduction of desktop publishing, several Univers fonts were deliberately altered in their conversion to digital form by software manufacturers. In particular, the desktop versions of Univers 47, 57, and 67 are considerably wider than their originals, consequently weakening the contrasts between different widths. Nevertheless, Univers remains, in my opinion, unequalled for its completeness, versatility, and aesthetic distinction. Especially in the late 20th century when novelty is unhesitatingly embraced and typefaces can be created on a whim, it is hard to imagine a typeface so thoroughly conceived and executed as Univers.

Univers, of course, is not the only typeface suitable for use in typographic design. Variety is necessary – and desirable. Choosing a typeface is a process of elimination based on whether the macro- and microaesthetic qualities of the typeface are appropriate to the purpose of the communication and its context of use. Even after carefully considering all of these factors, though, a number of typefaces might be suitable for any given problem. Ultimately, the final choice of typeface is a question of personal preference and taste.

All typefaces serve fundamentally the same purpose: to communicate. The purpose behind the communication – for example, to inform, to entertain, or to persuade – is expressed, in part, by the typeface chosen. As the communication objectives change, so might the typeface.

Depending on its context of use, different criteria must be applied when selecting a typeface. When used in display size on a poster, typefaces are evaluated on purely aesthetic criteria: how the qualities of the letterforms, in that particular size, interact for that particular set of words.

When used for continuous text, both aesthetic and functional criteria come into play. Legibility then becomes the key consideration.

The criteria of legibility require that extra attention be paid to the specific letterforms of the typeface. Reading is a dynamic process in which all letterforms have equal value: each letterform must integrate unobtrusively into the flow of words. Because letterforms with too much individuality and character distract the reader, a typeface with too many idiosyncrasies or unusual letterforms will, most likely, not work for continuous text. Typefaces that appear more legible than others share certain characteristics such as harmony, simplicity, and dignity, qualities that are difficult to determine and quantify.

On the macroaesthetic level, a typeface is evaluated on the form and counterform of its letters, their combination in words, and the relative size of its upper and lower case. Microaesthetically, the focus is on the tapering of curves, the connection of strokes, the form of serifs, and the proportions of ascenders and descenders. In financial communications, for instance, the choice of a particular typeface may be determined by the form of the numerals. All of these subtle nuances in the design of letterforms contribute to the reason for preferring one typeface to another.

A typeface should always be evaluated in the size, type of composition, and, if possible, the color it is to be used in. A single-line type specimen is insufficient to determine the suitability of a typeface. For the same reason, it is impossible to judge typographic design based on a sketch which does not show the nuances of letterform details, size, interline space and line breaks. One of the benefits of computer technology is that it allows easy examination of these details while the project is still in the development phase.

The immense number of available typefaces tempts designers to use type style as a crutch. Typeface itself, they assume, will rescue a weak and flaw-ridden composition; conversely, a bad typeface will be blamed for a poor solution. Good typographic design depends less on the chosen typeface than on arrangement, size, line length, letter, word and interline space. Mediocre typography is caused mainly by confusion and incompetence in working with these variables, not bad typefaces. Using a novelty typeface will not save poor typographic design any more than a classic typeface will. With skill and imagination, an unusual typeface can indeed yield interesting results; still, it is better in the end to use a limited selection of proven typefaces diligently and with intelligence than to rely on novelty faces that inevitably lead to results that soon look dated.

Original Univers font matrix, conceived by Adrian Frutiger, Paris, 1956.

A

*The character of all upper
and lower case letters is
determined by the letter's
structure, a series of
vertical, horizontal, slanted,
and curvilinear strokes.
The capital A, for instance,
is made up of two
slanted strokes and one
horizontal stroke.*

The form of letters

Each of the upper and lower case letters is unique because of its distinct structure. The upper case letter A, for example, derives its character from its strong triangular shape consisting of three distinct strokes – not from being light or bold, wide or narrow, roman or italic, sans serif or serif.

Typographic communication relies primarily on the structure of letters. Letterforms, therefore, should be clear and concise, unencumbered by details.

Equally important for communication are the relationships between letters, as the intrinsic visual quality of each letter changes when placed in context with other letters. A well-designed typeface allows the weight of strokes and curves, the counterforms, and the spacing between letters to coordinate into a virtually unlimited number of combinations.

The basic forms of letters can be seen as a code that is effective only if known to the reader. Drastic changes in form and structure hamper the reader's ability to differentiate between letters. Changes in form thus can only be microaesthetic changes: subtle intrusions into established norms. The challenge for the typeface designer is to expand on the accepted norm without destroying the identity of the individual letter.

	–	EFHILT	fijlt
	/	MNKY	k
/		VWX	vwxy
/	–	ZA	z
	)	BDGJPRU	abdghmnpqru
)	–	COQS	ceos

Each letter is a code that derives its meaning from a specific combination of vertical, horizontal, slanted and curvilinear strokes.

The upper half is more essential to the identity and recognition of a letter than the lower half.

Aa Bb Cc Dd
Ee Ff Gg Hh
Ii Jj Kk Ll
Mm Nn Oo Pp
Qq Rr Ss Tt
Uu Vv Ww Xx
Yy Zz

Aa Bb Cc Dd
Ee Ff Gg Hh
Ii Jj Kk Ll
Mm Nn Oo Pp
Qq Rr Ss Tt
Uu Vv Ww Xx
Yy Zz

visual literacy

visual literacy

Case

A a

Face

A A

*Variations of letterforms
are subordinate to the
basic structure of the letter.*

Slant

A A

Weight

A A A A

Width

A A A A

Variations of letterform

The alphabet is used in countless different styles, all of them variations of basic letterforms. Most common are variations in case, face, slant, weight, and width.

Case. Each letter is used in two versions: upper case and lower case; of different forms yet identical meaning. Because of their uniform height and similar widths, capital letters are less differentiated than lower case letters, which are distinguished by ascenders, descenders, and more varied forms.

Face. Type is generally divided into two categories: serif and sans serif, though both share the same principles of form. The additional detail of serifs and the weight difference in the strokes and curves of individual letterforms provide visual character and can enhance the readability of continuous text.

Slant. Slant refers to the angle of type relative to the baseline. Roman type is characterized by vertical strokes. Italic type deviates from roman by 12 to 15 degrees.

Weight. Weight refers to the thickness of the strokes relative to their height. In regular weight, the width of the capital letter I is about one seventh its height. Regular weight is closer to light weight than to heavy.

Width. Width refers to a letter's proportion relative to its height. In a wide typeface, the negative white space (counterform) is larger in proportion to the positive form than in a narrow typeface. The compact, narrow negative spaces of condensed letterforms are more elegant than those in wide letters.

LITTLE   lift   photograph

WAX   wavy   photograph

GOOD   case   *photograph*

photograph

photograph

WE APPLY CRYPTOGRAPHY TO PROTECT

we apply cryptography to protect proprietary

A word composed of letters with horizontal and vertical strokes appears more rigid than a word consisting of predominantly curvilinear strokes. LITTLE, consisting of horizontal and vertical strokes, WAX, consisting of predominantly slanted strokes, and GOOD, consisting of predominantly round strokes, have entirely different appearances.

Variations in letterform change the semantic and syntactic quality of the word "photograph".

Lower case letters, with their ascenders and descenders, provide more varied word shapes than upper case letters.

The word

Every word is comprised of a particular set of letters, whose sequence and form makes each word semantically and syntactically unique. A word consisting of predominantly curvilinear letters differs greatly from one composed of angular letters.

Likewise, a word set in all upper case letters is distinct from the same word set in lower case. When set in all upper case, the word is more uniform in shape and considerably wider. Lower case letters, with their ascenders and descenders, provide more varied word shapes than upper case letters, making them easier to identify and read. Because text set entirely in upper case is strenuous to read, large quantities of continuous text are generally set in lower case with an upper case letter at the beginning of each sentence.

The visual and semantic quality of a word or text may be enhanced by variation in the case, face, slant, weight and width of the letterforms. For instance, the distinct slant of italics provides a word with a certain "flow" that roman type lacks. The subtle microaesthetic details of serifs in the individual letterforms contribute significantly to the visual quality of text.

sonic

sonic

Normal letterspace is related to the counterforms of lower case letters. Typefaces with large counterforms require more letterspace than typefaces with small counterforms.

Letterspace must be decisive, either in harmony with or in strong contrast to the counterforms of lower case letters.

For text, most typefaces set with the default set width appear too tight. Additional letterspace improves legibility and aesthetic quality.

Architecture of information

Architecture of information

Architecture of information

Architecture of information

Architecture of information

Architecture of information

A r c h i t e c t u r e   o f   i n f o r m a t i o n

A r c h i t e c t u r e   o f   i n f o r m a t i o n

Letterspace
(Track) 0

The architecture of information is determined on both the macro- and microaesthetic level

Letterspace
(Track) 2

The architecture of information is determined on both the macro- and microaesthetic level

Letterspace

The space between letters is integral to all typography. A particular letterspace may enhance or destroy the aesthetic quality of a typeface or the legibility of text. With the computer, choosing the letterspace is entirely at the discretion of the designer. Unprofessional typesetting is generally caused not by the choice of typeface, but by too much, too little, or irregular letterspacing. When letterspacing is too tight, the type appears patchy, disrupted by clusters; when too open, it looks scattered and fragmented. In both instances, the type is irritating and tiresome to read.

The correct letterspacing in a continuous text is a subtle question of balance: what is the optimum space that sufficiently separates the letters without creating a string of disconnected elements that are difficult to grasp?

The answer depends on the typeface and size, and the visual result intended by the typographic designer.

For both serif and sans serif type, the optimum letterspace for text is determined by the counterforms of the lower case letters. Typefaces with small counterforms require less space between letters than those with large counterforms. If the letterspace is visually larger than the median counterform of the lower case letters, the type appears too open.

On the computer, most design applications adopt an average set width intended to work with all type sizes. For most typefaces, however, text composed with this setting appears too tight, requiring the letterspace to be increased for optimum legibility and aesthetic quality.

Assemblage

Letterspace
(Track) 0

Assemblage

Letterspace
(Track) –5

*In sizes larger than
24 point, most typefaces
set with the average
set width value appear
too open. Reduced letter-
spacing improves
their aesthetic quality.*

*The visual quality of
a word set in all capital
letters is considerably improved by kerning.
Left: Default spacing,
unkerned.
Right: Visually corrected
spacing, kerned.*

PANTHEON   PANTHEON

In sizes larger than 24 point, most typefaces composed
   with an average set width appear too open. Display sizes
   generally require a decrease in letterspacing.
In large type sizes, individual letterforms are visually more
   distinct, making it important to pay special attention to the
   letterforms in relation to each other. Visually awkward
   combinations, such as Ke, LT, ey, vo, are improved by
   reducing the space between the individual letters.
   Adjusting the letterspace between two letters is known
   as kerning.
Words set in all capital letters also require attention to the
   space between individual letters. The particular combinations of letterforms determine whether space needs
   to be added or subtracted to achieve a visually even
   composition.

The optimum letterspace for a word set in all capital letters
   is determined by letters with large counterforms, such as
   C, D, G, O, Q, or with large surrounding space, such
   as L, T, V, W, Y. If any of these letters stand apart, the space
   between the other letters needs to be increased. Ultimately, every letter should unobtrusively integrate itself
   into the visual form of the word.

Word space
too tight

Merely visual space is Euclidean, that is, namely, continuous, homogeneous, connected and static. This was the result of the abstraction of the visual faculty from the other senses at the moment of the phonetic alphabet – the first and only time this ever happened in the world, i.e., the fifth

Word space
too open

Merely visual space is Euclidean, that is, namely, continuous, homogeneous, connected and static. This was the result of the abstraction of the visual faculty from the other senses at the moment of the phonetic alphabet – the first and only time this ever happened in the world

Word space should be slightly larger than the counterforms of lower case letters. Too little and too much space equally damage the legibility and aesthetic quality of text.

Word space is uniform only in type composed ragged right. In justified type, the variation in word space from line to line should not be noticeable.

Normal
word space
for text

Merely visual space is Euclidean, that is, namely, continuous, homogeneous, connected and static

i   i   i i   i i   i   i   i   i i   i

Merely visual space is Euclidean, that
is, namely, continuous, homogeneous, connected and static. This was the result of

Merely visual space is Euclidean, that is,
namely, continuous, homogeneous, connected and static. This was the result of the

Word space

A carefully composed line of type appears as a continuous, even string of words separated by unobtrusive, visually uniform space. Too much word space creates a fragmented appearance; too little space causes insufficient separation between the words for comfortable reading.

For text, the normal word space is approximately the width of the lower case i. However, the optimum word space depends on the counterforms of the lower case letters. A typeface with small counterforms requires less word space than one with large counterforms. In larger type sizes, the word space should be decreased in accordance with the letterspace.

Uniform word space can only be achieved with ragged right setting. In justified type, extra space must be distributed between the individual words, resulting in word spaces that vary from line to line.

Because of the noticeable differences in word space, justified type often appears uneven and erratic, especially when set to a narrow column width. Consistent and uniform word space is more important than equal line length. A text with even word spacing is more pleasant to read, not being hampered by the irregularities inherent in justified text. If justified text is required, words should be hyphenated whenever necessary to avoid excessive word space.

To achieve a visually consistent composition, word space should be slightly reduced after commas and periods.

Merely visual space is Euclidean,
that is, namely, continuous,
homogeneous, connected and static.
This was the result of the
abstraction of the visual faculty

Merely visual space is Euclidean, that is, namely, continuous,
homogeneous, connected and static. This was the result of the abstraction of the visual faculty from the other senses at the moment of
the phonetic alphabet – the first and only time this ever happened in
the world, i.e., the fifth century B.C. In the electric simultaneous

Merely visual space is Euclidean, that is, namely, continuous, homogeneous, connected and
static. This was the result of the abstraction of the visual faculty from the other senses at the moment
of the phonetic alphabet – the first and only time this ever happened in the world, i.e., the fifth
century B.C. In the electric simultaneous time, we are encompassed by the new electric space which
is simultaneous and acoustic, i.e. we hear from all directions at once creating a space which is

Merely visual space is Euclidean, that is,
namely, continuous, homogeneous,
connected and static. This was the result
of the abstraction of the visual faculty from
the other senses at the moment of the

Merely visual space is Euclidean, that is,
namely, continuous, homogeneous,
connected and static. This was the result
of the abstraction of the visual faculty from
the other senses at the moment of the

$1/7$

$1/5$

*Composed in the same
type size and with the same
interline space, a narrow
column of text appears
more open than a wide
column. To achieve a gray
value similar to the
narrow column, the inter-
line space of the wide
column would have to be
increased.*

*For text, the interline
space measured from the
baseline to the x-line
should not be less than the
height of the capital H.*

*In a good ragged right
composition, the difference
between the longest and
the shortest line is approximately one fifth to one
seventh of the total column
width. Paragraphs should
start with a short line,
followed by a long line. To
achieve an even, yet
visually active rag, hyphen-
ations are mandatory.*

Interline space

A carefully composed column of text appears as a series of
lines separated by horizontal bands of white space.
To guide the eye effortlessly across each line, and to facili-
tate the transition from one line to the next, the interline
space must be visually larger than the space between
words. For text to be legible, the interline space, measured
from the baseline to the x-line of the line below, should
never be less than the height of the capital H.
Interline space is inextricably linked to line length and the
x-height of the typeface used. Composed in the same size
and with the same interline space, short lines appear
more open than long lines; similarly, given the same size
and interline space, a typeface with a small x-height
appears to have more interline space than a typeface with
a large x-height. The wider the line and the larger the

x-height, the more space that is needed to separate
the individual lines of type visually.
If space is limited, a smaller type size composed with
a small interline space is preferable to a slightly larger
type size set solid.

M	6 pt
M	7
M	8
M	9
M	10
M	11
M	12

*The standard point sizes
for text and display type.*

M	14 pt
M	16
M	18
M	20
M	24

M	30 pt
M	36
M	42
M	48
M	60

Type size

The standard type sizes used today originated in metal
  typesetting. Although any type size can be created on the
  computer, a limited range of sizes is preferable for
  effective work. A concise, calibrated range of sizes helps
  to establish ratios between type size, interline space,
  and the typographic structure.

Type sizes are generally divided into text sizes and display
  sizes, specified in points: 12 points = 1 pica; 72 points =
  6 picas = 1 inch. The point size is only an indication of the
  actual visual size of type; at the same point size, a typeface with a large x-height will look bigger than a typeface
  with a small x-height.

The choice of a particular size is determined by the intended
  design, the nature of the information, legibility and
  function, and the dimensions of the available space.

The standard sizes for text type are 6, 7, 8, 9, 10, 11,
  12 point; the sizes for display type are 14, 16, 18, 20, 24, 30,
  36, 42, 48 and 60 point. Larger sizes are determined as
  required.

Continuous text is most efficiently read when set in a medium
  type size of approximately 9 point. At that size, the
  eye captures groups of 8 to 10 letters simultaneously.
  At larger sizes, the number of letters captured decreases,
  slowing down reading. Efficient reading also depends
  on a comfortable line length of 40 to 60 characters,
  and adequate interline space and physical conditions such
  as environment and lighting, and, most importantly,
  the reader's motivation.

The visual size of type
is determined by the x-height
of lower case letters.

9/12 pt Univers 55

The visual size of type
is determined by the x-height
of lower case letters.

9/12 pt Bodoni

*Set in the same point
size, two typefaces may
appear different in
size, depending on their
x-height.*

	.375 pt
	.5
	.75
	1
	1.5
	2
	3
	4
	6

Rule weight

The weight of a rule is measured in points. The most common
rule weights are .375, .5, .75, 1, 1.5, 2, 3, 4 and 6 point.
Although on the computer rules can be created in any
weight, it is more efficient to work with a standard set that
can be easily recalled.

The choice of a particular weight is determined by its intended
function and visual effect. The visual appearance of a
rule depends, in part, on its length – a short rule appears
heavier than a long rule of the same weight.

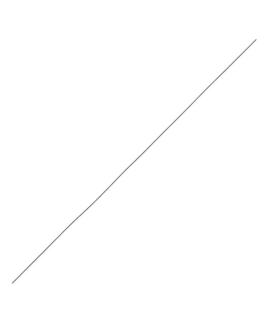

Dots, placed at decreasing intervals, form a visual line.

A horizontal line is stable. The two ends emphasize its direction.

The strongest contrast to a horizontal line is a vertical line. A vertical line, unlike a horizontal line, is unstable. Its quality seems to be dictated by gravity.

Depending on the angle, a slanted line is more or less unstable.

Line elements

A line, in essence, can be perceived as dot in motion: the static quality of the dot, as it becomes a line, is transformed into dynamic movement. By nature, the length of a line is infinite, its weight undefined, its direction undetermined.

In typographic design, a line assumes different functions: it may, for example, organize, structure, connect, separate, emphasize, highlight or enclose. In typography, lines stand clearly apart. Their visual qualities are very different from type, and their presence is powerful.

When using lines, questions related to weight, length, direction, and form immediately arise. How long and what weight should the line be? Should it be straight, angled, or curved? When does the line cease to be a line and become a plane?

Highly adaptable, a line invites experimentation, possibly in the form of a loosely sketched letter or a study in rhythm. In any case, it is a dynamic element that is essential in bringing ideas to life.

A

A

An imaginary line appears between two elements that are in an uninterrupted, direct relationship to one another. A sense of space and direction is established by their presence. Depending on the proximity and weight of the elements, visual lines assume different degrees of importance.

A

In typographic design there are two types of line:
the concrete line and the imaginary (visual) line. Length,
weight, and direction characterize the concrete line.
The imaginary, visual line occurs between two or more
elements. This type of line is an extraordinarily important
aspect of typographic design.

Two lines of different direction, when connected, create an angle, which begins to define a two-dimensional space. Unlike a straight line, which is defined by its two end-points, the angled line is characterized by three points.

Angled lines contrast strongly with typography, which is predominantly horizontal and vertical.

A stepped line, consisting of horizontals and verticals, echoes the horizontal and vertical characteristics of typography.

A curved line is expansive.
It has a radiant quality
that is increased by the
points of tension on both
ends. A curved line con-
trasts strongly with the predominant horizontals and
verticals of typography.

A spiral appears infinite,
moving simultaneously in
opposite directions, inward
and outward.

A wavy line is soft and
fluid; it appears unreliable
and ephemeral.

The visual identity of
a line is defined by the
surrounding space.
Separated by space, lines
appear as figures against
a background. Reducing
the space causes the
lines to merge into a grey
value, dissolving the
character of the individual
lines.

The visual character of a
line depends on the
proportion of its length to
its width. If the width
is substantially increased,
the line loses its vitality
and turns into a static
plane. A thin line appears
to be moving faster,
visually, than a bold line.

Two parallel bold lines
produce a thin negative
line. The two bold
lines seem to press down
upon the negative line.

A line consisting of
individual dots or dashes
has more visual
energy than a solid line
of the same weight.

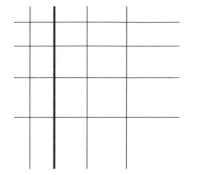
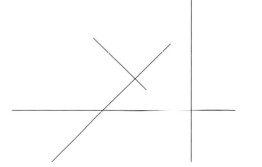

*Combining different
weights, breaking, repeat-
ing, crossing, shifting,
and slanting change the
expression of lines.*

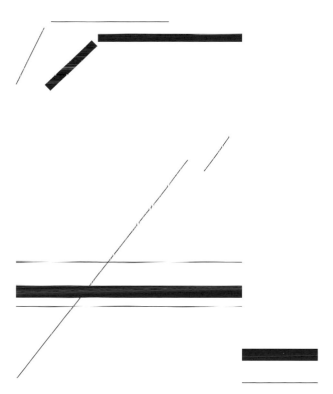

The circle, square, and equilateral triangle are the three basic geometric elements.

The circle is stable, its orientation neutral. In horizontal or vertical orientation, the square and equilateral triangle are stable; when slightly rotated they are unstable.

Changing one dimension transforms the square into a rectangle. A horizontal rectangle appears heavier than a vertical one of the same size.

Geometric elements

The basic geometric elements are the square, circle, and equilateral triangle. Through combining, cutting and distorting these elements, an unlimited number of new shapes can be created. Each of the basic geometric elements is symmetrical in shape, with a distinct character that can be easily memorized, making them versatile components for visual messages and symbols. The meaning of many traffic and hazard signs worldwide, for example, is linked to these shapes.

A geometric element is perceived relative to the space it is placed in as a plane or as a dot. Depending on its surroundings, it may be perceived as a dot next to large elements; next to small elements as a plane.

The orientation and expression of the circle are fixed. The square and equilateral triangle assume different visual qualities depending on their orientation. The square, with its horizontal base and two vertical sides, is stable. Rotated between 0 and 45 degrees, it appears unstable. The equilateral triangle with a horizontal base is stable. Rotated between 0 and 60 degrees, it appears unstable.

Cutting, removing, shifting and distorting can yield an unlimited number of new shapes, each with its own characteristics.

Purchase Order

Seller	Ship to CCC	No.
		Date
		Terms
	Invoice in Triplicate to this Address	
Ship via	Delivery required at Destination	FOB
Show CCC Seller Code	Commodity Code	And our Order Number on your Invoice
Quantity	Unit	Description	Price

Subject to Federal Excise Tax	Subject to State Sales Tax	Subject to City Sales Tax
A Packing Slip must accompany all shipments	Charge Account No.	Requisitioned by
Immediate Attention Acceptance of this order is subject to the terms and conditions on the reverse side.	By:	**Continental**

As structural elements, lines can establish a hierarchy
   to guide the reader through the information presented.
   In this case, the lines are purely functional, with no
   other meaning attached to them.
Lines can act as transitional elements from ideas to
   representations: abstract concepts can be made visual
   by lines. A single arrangement can have many
   meanings, providing a rich source of expression.
When an identifiable object is portrayed, the line
   is representational, its meaning tied to the object or
   event and its connotations.

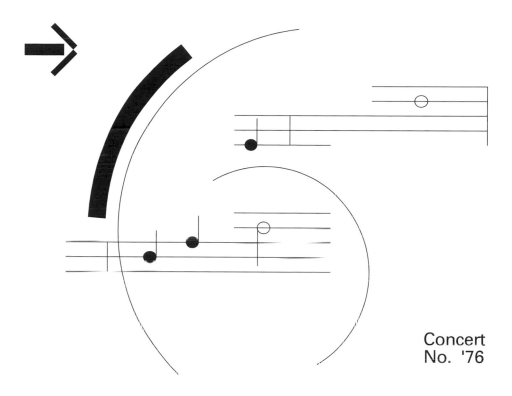

Concert
No. '76

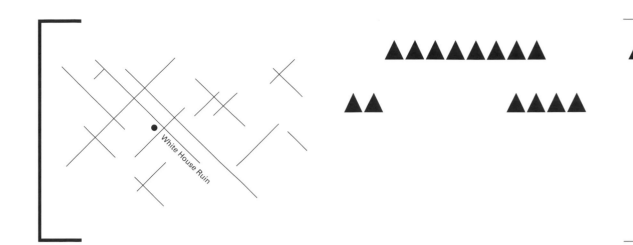

White House Ruin

Canyon de Chelly

Mummy Cave

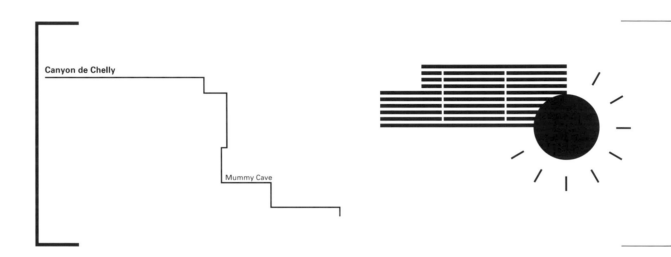

Escalante Desert

Geometric elements and lines have inherent semantic qualities conducive to illustrating visual ideas.

Connotative maps of Arizona landscapes for an essay about the petro-glyphs of North American Indians. Lines, circles, and triangles are used to visualize canyons, mountains, deserts, salt lakes, and other natural landmarks.

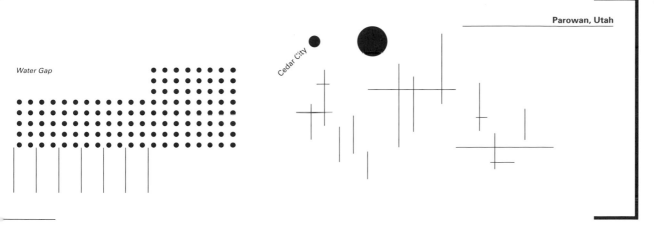

Water Gap

Cedar City

Parowan, Utah

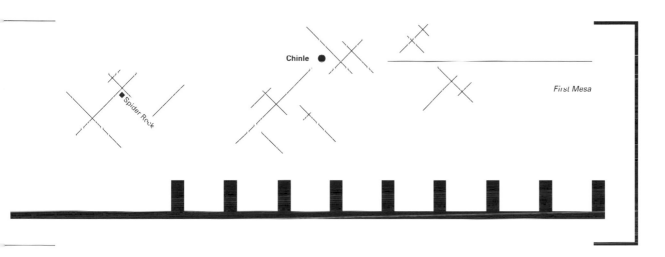

■Spider Rock

Chinle

First Mesa

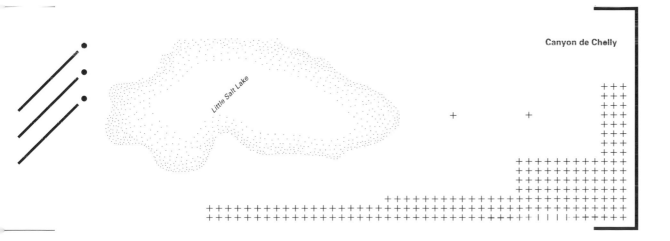

Little Salt Lake

Canyon de Chelly

*Connotative map of
Union Square in New York
City. A capital U com-
bined with a black square
alludes to the shape of
the park. Lines and geo-
metric elements suggest
the surrounding city.*

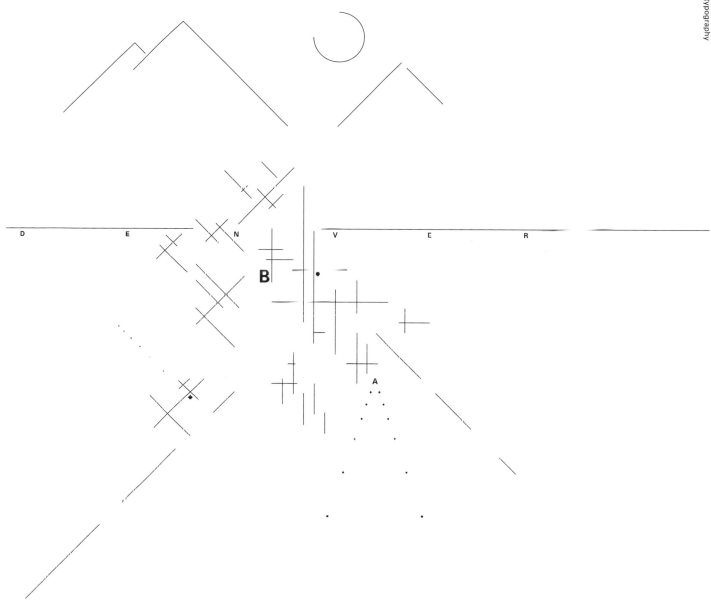

Are these examples still typography or are they
    graphic illustrations based on typographic elements?
    The term typography becomes ambiguous at
    this point. Does typography ever end and transform
    into graphic design?
In working with typographic materials, no such distinction
    can, or should, be made. Every design problem must
    be approached as a typo-graphic one.

*Lines serve as
illustrative elements for
a connotative map
of Denver, Colorado.*

2

Aspects of design

Typographic design is both process and product – a creative combination of communication practice and aesthetic theory. It begins with the selection and arrangement of typographic elements to communicate a message, and it ends with a composition in two-dimensional space.

The established principles of typography could be likened to the principles underlying architecture or music – necessary for craft but insufficient for art. Vitruvius and Bach, although masters of their craft, possessed something unquantifiable which made their work special: lifelong commitment, unique talent, inspiration and passion.

The sensitive, accomplished typographic designer must take into account not only the purpose of any given design, but also those technical and economic conditions which simultaneously limit and realize the work.

Space

In typographic design, typographic elements
and two-dimensional space interact with one
another in a figure/ground relationship.
This relationship between typographic form
and its background is fundamental to
design. Equal consideration must be given to
each: the interaction between them is
mutual and mutable.

Space is the common ground for all elements;
it provides a frame of reference and
significantly affects the expressive qualities
of the elements placed within it. Depending on their placement within a given space,
the same elements will assume different
visual aspects of weight and movement.
The visual expression of space is determined
by both the characteristics and the placement of elements within it.

Space is visually subdivided by the tension
that develops between an element and the
boundaries of the space. Inherent in
every text, typeset or handwritten, is a basic
shape that is determined by the size,
spacing, and organization of elements. The
shape of the negative space always develops
from the composition of these elements.

Space has two fundamental characteristics:
size and proportion. Rectangular space and
square space are delineated by two horizontals and two verticals, which determine
its size and proportion. A square, because of
its equal horizontal and vertical delin-
eations, is visually neutral. A rectangular
space has specific visual forces – horizontal
space is passive, vertical space is active.

In most cases, the size and proportion of
space are determined at the beginning of a
project, and unlike the size, weight, and
form of elements, are usually not changed
thereafter.

*In typographic design,
space is defined by two
horizontals and two
verticals, which may be
the edges of a page
or a frame. Blank space
contains unlimited
possibilities of design.*

Space is an ambiguous
quantity: two or three lines
form a weak space. A space
loosely defined by two
vertical lines appears taller
than a space defined by
horizontal lines. A fourth
line articulates the space
precisely.

52

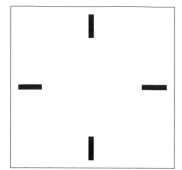

Square, horizontal,
and vertical spaces all have
unique visual qualities.
These qualities can be used
to reinforce the semantic
properties of the commu-
nication. A square is
visually stable; horizontal
and vertical space suggest
expanse.

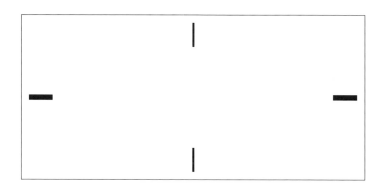

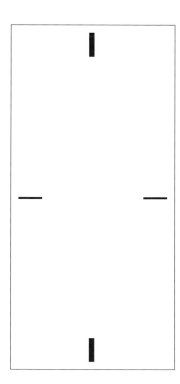

M

Space can be imagined
without elements,
but elements cannot exist
without space. Space
provides the frame of
reference for typographic
elements. In space, the
size of elements becomes
relative: two identical
elements appear differently
depending on the
size of the space they are
placed in.

The tension between the
elements and the bound-
aries of space visually
subdivides space. Depend-
ing on its placement in
relation to the boundaries,
a typographic element
assumes different visual
qualities. The visual
subdivision of space is vital
to all typographic design.

V
N
O
A

The character of individual letters is pronounced when they are separated by distinct spaces. The individual character is de-emphasized, once they are combined into a word.

In typography, space is the most common means of visual organization. For example, we recognize a word because of the space that groups a series of letters. Lines of type are more or less pronounced depending on the space between them.

A
NO
V

NOVA

Letters placed at random on a background appear as individual forms. When arranged in a particular sequence to form a word, their individual identity is subsumed.

The spatial relationships between letters is important to legibility. Too little space causes the letters to overlap, creating a cluster of forms. Too much space creates a string of individual elements that are difficult to read.

When words are grouped into sentences, they begin to form a texture, created by the lines of type and the space between them.

The blank space between letters, words, and lines is vital to all typographic design. Through the slightest increase or decrease of space between the typographic elements, the designer determines the visual quality of a composition.

Merely visual space is Euclidean, that is, namely, continuous, homogeneous, connected and static. This was the result of the abstraction of the visual faculty from the other senses at the moment of the phonetic alphabet – the first and

Merely visual space is Euclidean, that is, namely, continuous, homogeneous, connected and static. This was the result of the abstraction of the visual faculty from the other senses at the moment of the pho-

Merely visual space is Euclidean, that is, namely,

continuous, homogeneous, connected and

static. This was the result of the abstraction of the

visual faculty from the other senses at the

moment of the phonetic alphabet – the first and

Merely visual space is Euclidean,

that is, namely, continuous, homoge-

neous, connected and static. This

was the result of the abstraction of

the visual faculty from the other

Letter-, word, and interline space contribute to the legibility and readability of text. Small differences in space can make a text pleasant or difficult to read.

Column one: regular letter- and word space; increasing interline space. Too little or too much interline space diminishes legibility.

Column two: increased letter-, word, and interline space; in all four examples the legibility is severely affected.

Merely visual space is Euclidean, that is, namely,

continuous, homogeneous, connected and

static. This was the result of the abstraction of the

visual faculty from the other senses at the

moment of the phonetic alphabet – the first and

Merely visual space is Euclid-

ean, that is, namely, continuous,

homogeneous, connected and

static. This was the result of the

abstraction of the visual faculty

Merely visual space is Euclidean, that is, namely,

continuous, homogeneous, connected and

static. This was the result of the abstraction of the

visual faculty from the other senses at the

moment of the phonetic alphabet – the first and

Merely visual space is

Euclidean, that is, namely,

continuous, homogeneous,

connected and static.

This was the result of the

*A space becomes visually
active when it is sub-
divided. The number, size
and proportion of the
subdivisions determine the
quality of space. A space
subdivided into equal units
is monotonous.*

*When differing values
are added, the spatial
qualities change. Each unit
appears to be on a sepa-
rate visual level, advancing
or receding in space.
The same visual principle
applies when the grey
values are created by text,
photographs and other
visual elements.*

A space subdivided into units of different size and proportion is visually more exciting and stimulating than a space subdivided into equal units. In space subdivided into different units, the points of alignment are distinct, each unit is in a unique relationship to adjacent units. The contrast of size and proportion between the individual units makes the space more engaging and increases the attention span of the viewer.

The examples shown here are only a few of the multiple possible variations based on nine units of different size and proportion.

Structure

A fundamental structure is inherent in all typography. Even a single word or line of type placed on a blank sheet of paper subdivides the space and creates a simple visual structure. Because a structure is always present to some degree, it serves as a powerful element in design.

Typographic design can proceed from two types of structure: an optically improvised visual structure, or a predetermined structure – the grid system.

An optically improvised visual structure results from arranging typographic elements according to aesthetic criteria. The size and shape of letters, words, and lines of type determine the subdivision of space. Like building blocks, the individual elements are highly dependent on each other: if one element is changed, other elements need to be adjusted, either in placement or size, to balance the composition. Since there are virtually no limitations to the arrangement of a given set of typographic elements, this visual structure is essentially an open system.

Typographic design based on empirical criteria is a personal expression of the designer, and demands creativity, sensitivity, intuition and judgment. To maintain design integrity, the designer must be constantly involved throughout the entire design and production process. This improvised visual approach can yield interesting and unique solutions.

For complex, extensive assignments, a predetermined structure – the grid system – is necessary. In contrast to the optically improvised structure, the grid is a closed system that is implemented consistently once the structure has been developed.

Modular grids consist of a series of modules separated by a consistent space and organized into columns and rows. Modules determine the dimensions and placement of graphic and typographic elements, which may include pictures, headings, text, captions, and page numbers. In this way, the grid serves as a strong organizational device, providing unity between page elements and the pages themselves, while at the same time allowing for a vast number of variations.

The grid functions strictly as an organizational device, one that provides order but is itself invisible. Graphic and typographic elements are guided by, but never subordinated to, the grid. Although it facilitates order, using a grid does not necessarily yield unimaginative and rigid solutions. Like any systematic approach, it can lead to lively results if used with imagination and applied to the right task.

Grid systems also make it easier for several individuals to collaborate on a large project. The design of a publication, for instance, is frequently a team effort, and benefits from the organized structure a grid system provides.

Working with a grid involves two phases: developing a structure that accommodates all the elements, and organizing those elements following that structure. Each phase is equally important. When devising a grid, the designer must not only take into account the idiosyncrasies of the typographic material but also anticipate all the possible problems of working with the material, for example the cropping of photographs. For this reason, the development of a grid must always proceed from an analysis of all the visual material that will be included in the design: the more thoroughly the structure is related to the given material, the more rigorous the visual solution will be.

During the initial phase of a project it is often more productive to rely on intuition and visual judgment. Once the basic design has been established, a calculated, rational structure may be developed that accommodates all elements originally placed visually.

Gene Youngblood
Expanded Cinema
Introduction by R Buckminster Fuller
E P Dutton
$4.95

1

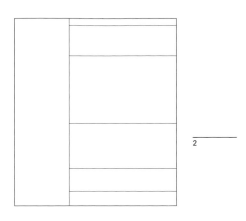

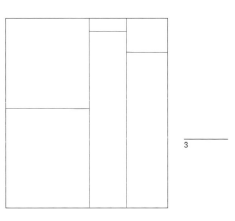

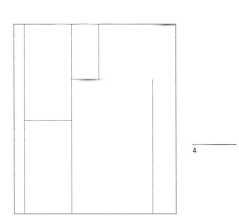

1 *Elements of information in a passive composition, with minimal differentiation between individual parts.*
2 *Visual structure; minimal interaction between information and space.*
3 *Visual structure; subdivided by different elements, space is active.*
4 *Visual structure with additional subdivisions of space.*

An optically improvised visual structure is derived from elements of information – it can not be created a priori. Developing a visual structure is often more difficult than the result suggests. Even a few elements allow so many possibilities of arrangement that it is often difficult to decide on the best solution.

To arrive at a meaningful solution, the designer must simultaneously address the visual and communicative aspects of design. Arranging elements based on purely visual principles might yield results that are aesthetically pleasing but do not communicate clearly. Structuring information visually is an excellent way to generate ideas in the initial phases of design. This spontaneous working method leads to concepts that may later be converted into a modular structure.

30 East Lane Avenue

Susan
Kaye
Zanin

Telephone
294 8777

Columbus
Ohio 43201

Julie Jamison

870
Greenridge Road

Colombus
Ohio 43011

Telephone
286
3726

2064 Indianola Columbus Ohio

43201

Anita Lamb

Telephone
291
6894

Ted Bailey

Telephone
242   5900

Columbus
Ohio
43210

161 Curl Drive

270 East 12th Avenue

Columbus

Ohio 43214

Thomas R. Melena

Telephone 885 9850

Telephone 294 5417

134 East 15
Avenue

Columbus Ohio

43201

Lynn Tabacchi

Susan B. Spero

200 East 17th Avenue

Telephone
294
5243

Columbus

Ohio 43601

345 E 13th Avenue

Columbus
Ohio
43210

Arnie Friedlander

316 6466

Telephone

Cindy Kerr   Telephone   4

2

4

Columbus
Ohio 43210

5356

High Street

North

179

Paul Leopold

E. Northwood, Apt. F

360

Columbus
Ohio

43201

286 3726

Telephone

These examples from a course in introductory typography at Ohio State University demonstrate some of the many possible ways a simple set of information can be visually organized.

The students were asked to compose their name, address, and telephone number in 14 point Univers 55. A 6 x 6 inch space was used to structure information based on the following constraints:
a. horizontal type only.
b. horizontal and vertical type combined.

c. horizontal, vertical, and diagonal type combined.
d. horizontal, vertical, diagonal, and circular type combined.
Through this study the students gradually became familiar with aspects of structuring space in typography. It also made them aware that even in a basic design problem a large number of plausible solutions can be generated. The study was strictly defined, allowing the students to concentrate on the arrangement of type.

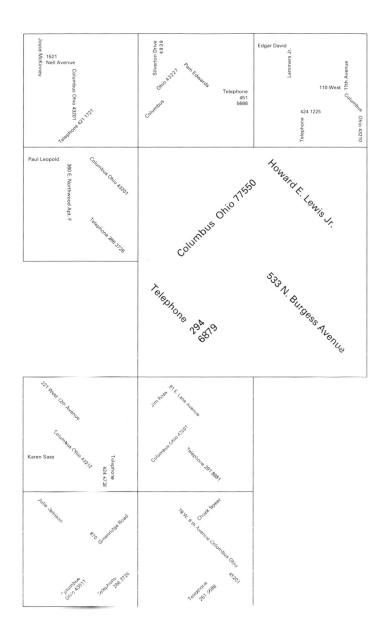

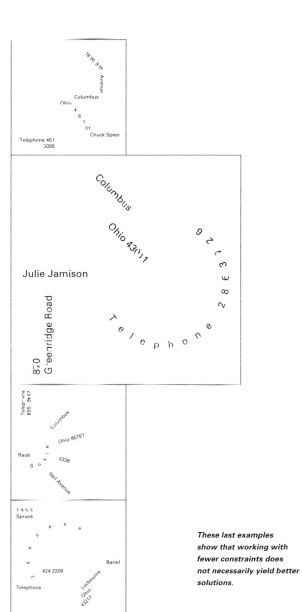

These last examples show that working with fewer constraints does not necessarily yield better solutions.

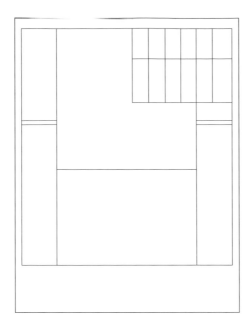

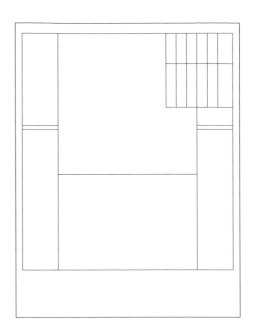

The design of this calendar, with photographs of Paris by Fredrich Cantor, is based on the combination of a predetermined and a visual structure.
The arrangement of the photograph, month name, and year on each page is part of the predetermined structure, while the arrangement of the weeks and days is decided by a variable structure of visual improvisation.
9 x 12 in

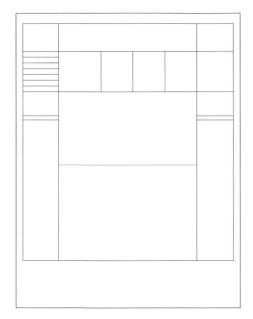

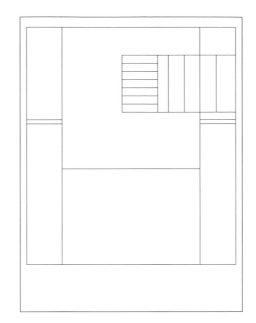

*Schematic drawings show
the predetermined structure
and the varying structure
combined.*

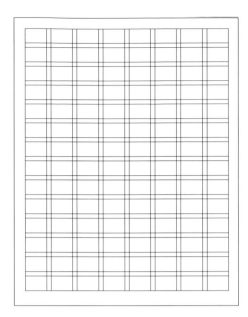

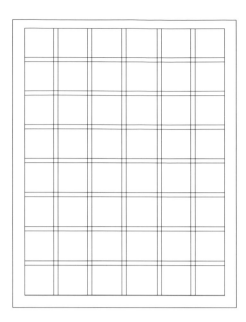

Modular grid for course descriptions on architecture programs.
8.5 x 11 in

Modular grid for exhibition reviews.
8.5 x 11 in

The modular grid is always tailored to the typographic requirements and visual material of a project. Every design problem is different and therefore requires a grid structure that can accommodate its particular elements. The challenge for the designer is to develop a structure with the appropriate number of subdivisions of space: too few limit the expressiveness of the design; too many increase the difficulty of work, even though they render an often necessary fineness of detail.

The modular grid is not just an organizational device for typographic elements. It is the key to a working method that increases efficiency in every phase of design, from selecting type size and interline space to composing the type, even to setting up templates and style sheets on the computer.

The modular grid is often blamed for stuffy, homogeneous design. In many instances, however, it is the designer who is ultimately at fault for a dull solution. The grid lends itself to use in many different ways, from strict adherence to playfully free interpretation.

For sequential, highly structured information, a hierarchical grid is often more appropriate than a modular grid. With a hierarchical grid, certain structural decisions are predetermined, making it easier to accommodate the various levels of verbal and visual information.

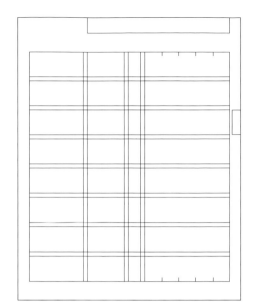

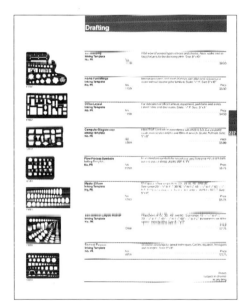

*Modular grid for an
exhibition catalog.
The three short vertical
lines at the top refer
to the substructure of
the section openers.
8.5 × 10 in*

*Hierarchical grid for
an art supply catalog with
over 1000 products.
The structure is deter-
mined by the various levels
of information. The four
short vertical lines at the
top and bottom refer
to the substructure in the
descriptive text.
9 × 11 in*

Introduction

The issues raised by Bat-
tery Park City are basic to
New York City's future,
from spatial planning to
the reconstruction of neigh-
borhoods.

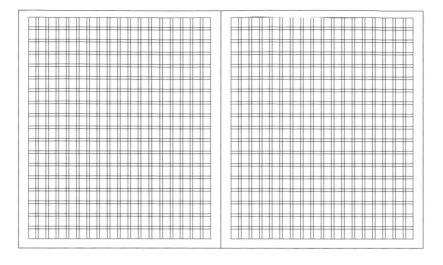

Design of **Abstract,**
a yearly publication of
studio projects and
research by students of
the Columbia University
Graduate School of
Architecture, Planning, and
Preservation, New York.
The information, such as
course title, project
description, and names
of students and studio
critics, remains essentially
the same each year.

The unusually finely-
detailed grid, consisting
of 18 x 18 units, allows
for many variations
of information structure.

8.5 x 10 in
160 pages
Black / white and
four-color process

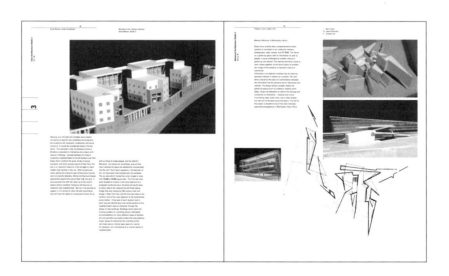

Double pages
from **Abstract 98-99.**

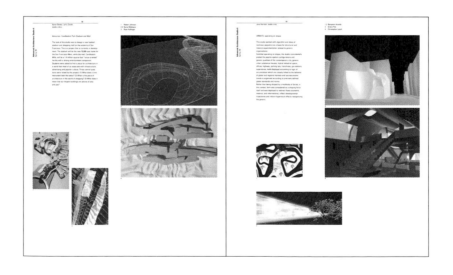

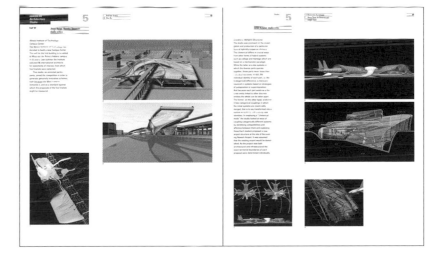

Double pages
from **Abstract 97-98.**

*Design of a monograph
for Nikken Sekkei,
planners, architects, and
engineers, Tokyo.
The book consists of three
parts, each with different
typographic requirements:
an illustrated history of
contemporary Japanese
architecture; an analysis of
24 selected projects; and an
extensive catalog of work
by Nikken Sekkei.*

*The 16 x 19 unit grid was
developed after a time-
consuming analysis of the
diverse visual material.
Text is set on six grid units,
captions on two. On text
pages, the top four units of
the outside column are
shifted inward two units,
creating a distinct space
for the page numbers.
On introductory pages,
which are always on the
right, this single shift
creates three distinct
spaces for the project title,
schematic drawing, and
page numbers.*

*10 x 10 in
288 pages
Four-color process*

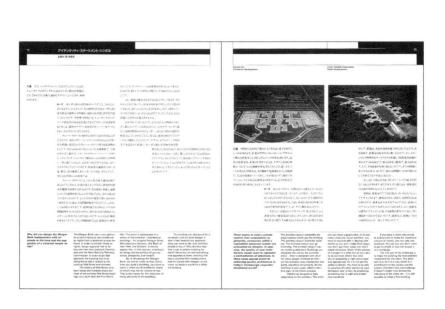

Design of **Kevin Roche:**
Seven Headquarters,
a book published by Office
Age for ITOKI, Tokyo.
The publication consists
of seven chapters, each
featuring a major corporate
headquarters designed by
the architect Kevin Roche.
Each chapter has four
sections: a general
description of the project;
the design process;
portfolio presentation;
and client interview.

The 12 x 9 unit grid was
developed after a thorough
analysis of all visual
materials, which included
more than 700 four-color
photographs and
English/Japanese text.
The typography takes
advantage of the many
structural possibilities
inherent in this unusually
finely-detailed grid.

9.375 x 11.375 in
216 pages
Four-color process

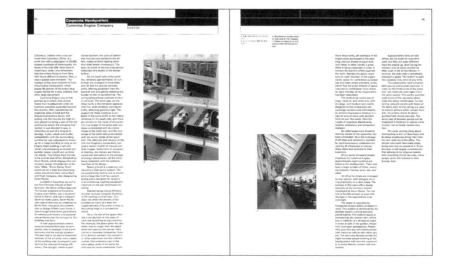

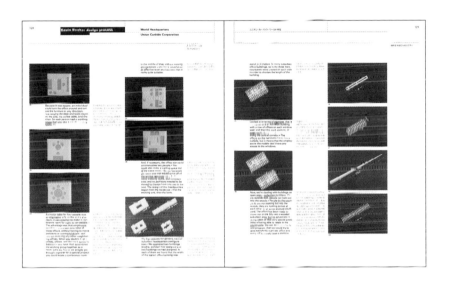

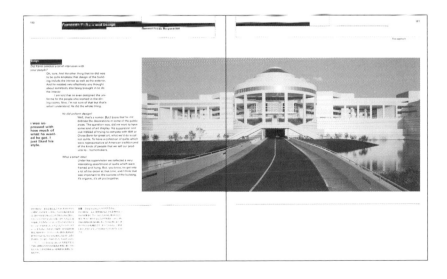

In many instances an elaborate structure is superfluous. An excess of possibilities, likewise, can be counterproductive in the layout process. A good typographic solution may require only a series of vertical align- ments and horizontal flow lines to provide visual continuity from page to page.

Four vertical alignments structure the information. The typographic variation follows from the nature of the text. 7.375 x 11 in

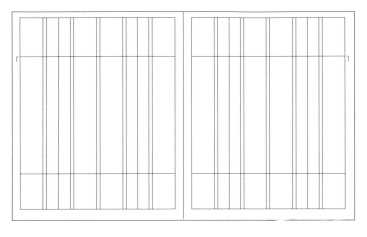

1

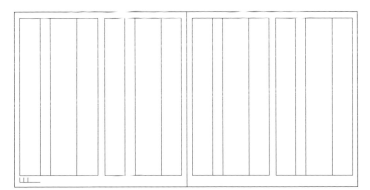

2

1 *Six columns and
two horizontal flow lines
structure text, subtitles,
footnotes, sideheads, and
running heads.*
8.5 x 10 in

2 *Three vertical alignments
structure text, subtitles,
and source of information.*
9 x 9 in

The design of Typography: Macro- and Microaesthetics is based on a grid consisting of 6 x 8 units. Each unit, measuring 6.5 x 6.5 picas, is subdivided into half units of 2.75 x 2.75 picas. The space between all units is 1 pica.

The margins on the left hand pages are 2.5 picas on the outside, 4.5 picas on the inside, 2.5 picas at the top, and 3 picas at the bottom.
On the right hand pages the margins are 4.5 picas on the inside, 2.5 picas on the outside, 2.5 picas at the top, and 3 picas at the bottom.

The interline space of all type is based on the height of a half unit (33 points) plus space between units (12 points).

This type
is set
with
11.25 point
interline space
so that
lines
5, 9, 13
etc.
correspond
with
the top
of a
grid unit.

This type
is set
with
9 point
interline
space
so that
lines
6, 11, 16
etc.
correspond
with
the top
of a
grid unit.

This type
is set
with
7.5 point
interline
space
so that
lines
7, 13, 19
etc.
correspond
with
the top
of a
grid unit.

ABCDEFGHIJKLMNOPQRSTUVWXYZ

E I L N

Sequence

Typographic communication depends on the
 sequence of letters, words, and sentences.
 Many words consist of the same letters,
 but it is the sequence of letters that determines the meaning of a word. Words
 arranged in a particular sequence form a
 sentence; a sequence of numerals creates
 a numeric value.
In typography, the basic sequence of elements
 is determined by the syntactic structure
 of language and grammar. Latin languages
 are generally read left to right, top to
 bottom, which influences the sequence
 of elements and creates a particular textual
 pattern.
Words and sentences can, however, be more
 than a series of elements horizontally
 aligned one after another. By increasing
 the space between letters and words, or by
 shifting the baseline of type, the visual
 expressiveness of typography can be significantly influenced. The space between
 elements becomes the vehicle for manipulat-
 ing and reinforcing typographic syntax. It
 is vital, however, that words and lines
 remain individual units that can be easily
 recognized.

EILN	ILNE	LEIN	NEIL
EINL	ILEN	LENI	NELI
ELNI	INEL	LINE	NILE
ELIN	INLE	LIEN	NIEL
ENIL	IELN	LNEI	NLEI
ENLI	IENL	LNIE	NLIE

NEIL

LINE   NILE
LIEN

LINE

NILE

*Every word consists of
a series of letters arranged
in a particular sequence.*

*Of the 24 possible
combinations of the letters
EILN, only four have a
specific meaning in English.*

*The sequence of letters
also determines the visual
qualities of a word.
Form and counterform
of adjacent letters merge,
creating a visual rhythm.*

LINE   LIN   LI   L   L   L   L
       E   NE INE   IN   I   N
                         E   NE   INE
                                      E

1

                                              E
                         E   NE   N
       E   NE   INE   IN   I   I
LINE   LIN LI   L   L   L   L

LINE   LIN   LI   L   L   L   L
       E   NE   INE   IN   I   I
                          F   NE   N
                                       E

2

              E
           N
L I N   E   I   L   N E
           L

3

L   I   I   E   L   N
         L N   I
N   E   E

---

1 2 3 Changes in sequence and letterspace affect the legibility and visual expression of words. 4 Legibility and expression are hampered by contrived arrangements.

4

TOKYO　**KYOTO**

Texas　**Taxes**

EARTH　**E**AR**TH**　E**ART**H

NIKKEN　**SEKKEI**

*1 2 Different words,
created by changing the
sequence of letters.
3 A sequence of letters
may be common to differ-
ent words.
4 Every word has special
idiosyncrasies. The logo-
type for Nikken Sekkei
takes advantage of the two
K's as the third and fourth
letter in each word.
Arranged side by side, the
two words seem to have
little in common.
Stacked one upon the
other, they form a unique
relationship because
of the sequence of letters.*

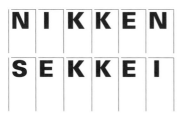

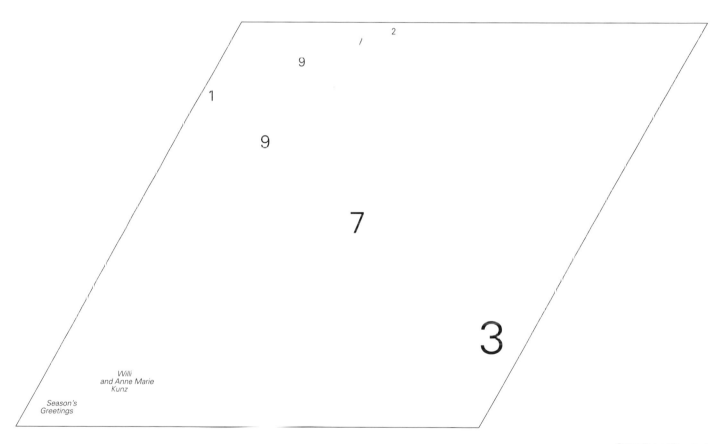

9136 9163 9316 9361 9613 9631
6139 6193 6319 6391 6913 6931
3169 3196 3619 3691 3916 3961
1369 1396 1639 1693 1936 1963

herzliche glückwünsche
zum neuen jahr
willi kunz
eisenwerkstrasse 31
frauenfeld

2
/
9
1
9
7
3

Willi
and Anne Marie
Kunz

Season's
Greetings

Season's greetings card
based on the 24 possible
sequences of four numbers.
8.25 x 4.125 in

Season's greetings card
with numbers arranged in
two different sequences,
reading in two directions.
The size of the numbers
and the intervals between
them connote time and
space. The visual concept –
1972 moving out, 1973
moving in – is enhanced by
the card's rhombic format.
5 x 5 in

LA   ON   SV
ax   ez   wb
lo   ye   si

Aa   Ee   Gg
Hh   Nn   Rr

Contrast of structure

Contrast

Typographic design depends on the contrast between elements. The most elementary contrast is that between the type and the background.

Every letterform is a composition of contrasting vertical, horizontal, diagonal, and curvilinear strokes. Its counterform is defined by the contrast with surrounding space. The typographic designer works with these contrasts.

The most significant contrasts in typographic design are the contrasts of form, weight, size, texture, and direction. Contrast of form, weight, and size can be established with the smallest typographic unit – the letter. Contrast of texture and direction encompasses several elements: words, lines of type, lines, or geometric elements.

The formal qualities of an element become more pronounced when the element is juxtaposed with a contrasting form, which then intensifies the visual qualities of both elements.

In a larger context, contrasts depend on the basic visual condition of the immediate presence of light. Light is effective only in contrast to dark, which subtracts from the visual force of light. Printing black on white, for instance, is subtractive: the added black subtracts white from the surface. A bold letterform subtracts more light from a surface than a light one.

Typography without contrast is lifeless and dull. Contrast is expressive: it may attract, stimulate, or challenge the reader, or intensify and articulate a visual statement. Contrasting elements are like reference points: they help establish a visual hierarchy and clarify communication. To be effective, contrasts must always be clear and decisive; they depend on omitting the extraneous that distracts from the essential.

Contrast of form

Letterforms vary in structure, width, slant, and face. All of these variations provide contrasts that are essential to typographic design.

Structure. Every word consists of a series of letters, each with a different structure. The contrasts of structure makes each word unique. For instance, the contrasts between the structure of letters in *film* are weak, in *keys* strong.

The difference of contrasts in upper and lower case letters is important for the legibility of text. The contrast of ascenders and descenders makes text composed in lower case letters visually more active than one in upper case. Contrast between upper case and lower case also provides important syntactic clues, such as signaling the beginning of a new sentence.

HH　　HH　　HH　　　　H*H*

_____
Contrast of slant

HH　　HH

HH

HH

_____
Contrast of width

_____
Contrast of face

Width. The limitation in width makes
　　effective contrast difficult to
　　achieve. Univers, with its several
　　distinct widths, is one of the
　　few typefaces which allow effective
　　contrast of width.

Slant. The difference between the
　　vertical strokes in a roman face and
　　the angled strokes in an italic
　　face provides an effective contrast.
　　This contrast is often used to
　　achieve semantic differences in a
　　text or to provide emphasis.

Face. The characteristics of a type-
　　face are highlighted when juxta-
　　posed with a contrasting face.
　　When two typefaces are used for
　　contrast, their forms must be
　　clearly different. Because of the
　　visual similarity of Univers
　　and Helvetica, combining these
　　typefaces would be senseless.

*Contrast of weight
between Univers 45, 55,
65, 75.*

AA   AA   **AA**

A**A**   A**A**

A**A**

Contrast of weight

Effective typography depends on the contrast of visual values, ranging from light to dark, created by the weight of type against a background. The visual texture of the page is formed by this contrast between different values.

When used for emphasis, weight differences must be distinct: values of weight which are too similar are ambiguous and ineffective.

Contrast of weight is not limited to type; it also comes into play between rules, photographs, and other visual elements. In establishing contrast between two elements, the intervening space becomes an important factor: when separated by excessive space, comparison is hampered, the contrast weak.

Size ratio 1:1.5 (6:9 pt)

Size ratio 3:4 (6:8 pt)

exploration
in communication

exploration
in communication

*Contrasts of size
with 6, 8, 9, 10, 12, 14 and
18 point Univers 55.*

Size ratio 1:2 (6:12 pt)

Size ratio 3:5 (6:10 pt)

exploration
in communication

exploration
in communication

Size ratio 1:3 (6:18 pt)

Size ratio 3:7 (6:14 pt)

Contrast of size

Inherent in the range of standard
type sizes (page 32) are many rational contrasts. Within a small
number of type sizes, for instance
6, 8, 9, 10, 12, 14 and 18 point are
ratios of 1:1.5, 1:2, 1:3, 3:4, 3:5, and
3:7, all of which are aesthetically
pleasing. Consideration of the
complete range of type sizes leads
to many other possibilities.
Establishing contrasts based on
mathematical ratios is only efficient
when working with the standard
size range. Arbitrary sizes,

measured in fractions of points,
are difficult to relate to one another.
Contrast of size then becomes a
purely visual decision.
To determine contrast of size, mathematical ratios provide guidance,
but do not replace sensitivity and
visual judgment.

*Contrast of texture
between capital letters,
medium grey text,
dark grey captions and
line pattern.*

*Contrast of texture
between headline, title,
text, square pattern,
and captions.*

C

T

J

B

I

Once again IBJTC's Trust Department had a record-setting year. In 1983 new trusteeships and fiscal agencies reached a volume in excess of $1.25 billion. The wide variety and complexity of the financings on which we were appointed as trustee and paying agent mirrored the innovations demanded by the marketplace. Euro-Bonds, Industrial Revenue Bonds, Pollution Control Bonds, and leveraged lease financings, appeared with such embellishments as floating rates, put options and stand-by letters of credit. Once again, our clients included such stellar names as Nissan, Hitachi and Japan Air Lines.

Expeditious processing of this new business and the day-to-day administration of an ever-growing portfolio of accounts has kept our staff among the best informed people in the field of corporate trust services. Anticipating a natural expansion of our customers' needs into other areas of Trust, we have been re-examining and expanding our capabilities in trusteeship, custody, escrow, and related functions to assure our ability to provide the widest range of services during 1984 and beyond. We face 1984 fully equipped to meet the needs of prospective debt issuers with top quality, timely and economical services.

IBJTC made significant progress in sophisticated lease arrangements during 1983, such as leveraged leasing for a wide range of industries.

An International
Viewpoint

Intergold publishes *Aurum*, a quarterly international magazine which covers a range of topics including market research, manufacturing technology, workshop techniques, comprehensive information on international exhibitions and events, retailing and marketing methods. In contrast to most jewelry magazines which concentrate on noteworthy international stories, *Aurum* takes an international overview of the world of gold jewelry. The magazine is always illustrated with a multitude of color photographs and is published in Geneva on the finest stock. *Aurum* is the communication vehicle for the Gold Fashion Trends Project, an essential source of gold information and necessary reading for anyone working with jewelry.

Aurum

is essential

reading

for anyone

working

with jewelry

Information about
subscriptions to *Aurum*
can be obtained
by contacting
the New York office:

International Gold
Corporation Limited
900 Third Avenue
New York, NY 10022
212 688 0005

Contrast of texture

Every typographic composition can be viewed as a texture, a pattern created by the repetition of elements. Form, size, and weight contribute to the character of texture, while the space between elements determines the visual density. Textures encompass an infinitely fine gradation of visual values, from light grey to nearly black. Each texture has a specific aesthetic dimension and depth.

A light grey texture appears more integrated with the background compared to a dark texture, which seems to separate from the background.

Every typeface has its own texture, grey value or "color." Futura Black has a very dense texture, Bodoni Regular a relatively transparent one. Through letter and interline space, the texture of a typeface can be changed. In contrast to text, single words set in a large point size display a coarse texture determined by the letterforms.

76

JICA Hokkaido International Centre

Building a Center for International Understanding

Location:
Obihiro City, Hokkaido

Site area:
4,391 m²

Building area:
2,132 m²

Total floor area:
4,400 m²

Building purpose:
Training facility

Number of floors:
+3, -1

Structure:
RC

Completed:
1996

Residence wing
and balconies viewed
from the courtyard.

*Contrast of direction
between horizontal text
and vertical title.*

*Contrast of direction
between vertical
alignment of type and
angled title.*

Building a Centre for International Understanding
Hokkaido is the second largest and most
northern of the four main islands of Japan.
Climatically and geographically, it's an area
of contradictions. Local weather patterns
are influenced by the marine triangle of the
Sea of Okhotsk, Japan and the Pacific,
creating many months of harsh winter offset
by cool, comfortable summers. The region
is home to several rare bio environments and
unique wilderness sites, from the Jozankei
Gorge to the Kushiro Swamps. Daisetsu
National Park and its mountains comprise
the backbone of the island. Sun and rich soils
make the area a prominent dairy and
crop-farming center, with farms run on an
extensive scale.

Located at a latitude of 43 degrees
north, the city of Obihiro is renowned
for the beauty of its scenery. During winter,
cold air masses move down from Siberia
and the temperatures drop to minus
30 degrees centigrade below zero while
summer temperatures can reach over
30 degrees centigrade.

Obihiro is the location of the Japan
International Cooperation Agency, (JICA)
that implements the programs of the Official
Development Assistance office (ODA).
JICA/Hokkaido International Centre is the
11th such ODA center and is founded on
"human development, national development
and unity among people" The Centre's
major focus is 'technology and knowledge

Bernard Tschumi
Dean

Columbia University
Graduate School of Architecture,
Planning, and Preservation

requests the pleasure
of your company for the

End-of-Year Exhibition

at Columbia University Architecture Galleries

Buell Hall and
Avery Hall 100, 400, 500
May 15-29

Saturday, May 15
6:00-8:00pm
reception and viewing

Contrast of direction

Contrast of direction is the most
explicit of contrasts. It encompasses
the entire composition of elements, including their surrounding
space, and can dramatically change
the visual expression of a word
or a line of type.

The horizontal movement of individual
words or lines of type contrasts
with their vertical alignment. When
type is set in narrow columns,
the vertical alignment becomes
stronger than the horizontal
movement of the individual lines.

In many instances, a word or
line element set vertically becomes
a structural element that subdivides space.

Typography, being dictated by reading
conventions, is predominately
horizontal/vertical, a schema
reinforced by the parallel boundaries of the format. Introduced
into this frame of reference, a
diagonal element creates strong
visual tension.

*Covers from a series of
type specimen books for
Typogram, New York.
The design is based on the
contrast of three type
sizes: the two initial letters
of the typeface featured
in each book are set large;
the full name of the
typeface is set medium;
and a listing of all typefaces
in each book is set small.
The underlying line
structure is derived from
the content's structure
and suggests the precision
of typesetting.*

*Desktop computers
give the designer access
to all typefaces in any
size, any width of compo-
sition and any interline
space. However, comparing
the type size and interline
space on the computer is
not as accurate and
convenient as it is with a
good type specimen book.
This page from the
Typogram Univers type
specimen book demon-
strates how size, weight,
and interline space
contribute to the textural
quality and grey value
of type.
8.75 x 12 in*

| Univers 55 | Adrian Frutiger, 1957 Haas'sche Schriftgießerei AG H. Berthold AG Typogram, New York | **Un** |

ABCDEFGHIJKLMNOP QRSTUVWXYZ123456 7890$&()!?.,-;:*""

abcdefghijkl mnopqrstuv wxyz

5 point
The space shuttle Challenger succeeded today in replacing defective electronics units on the crippled Solar Max satellite for the first ex

6 point
Before dawn the next morning we pulled away from Pakokku into the deserted gunmetal river and made for the anci

6.5 point
When you consider the question of money, you will find that it was handled differently in each case accordin

7 point
Kangaroos still loll in the shade of the gum trees at the Noosa golf club, as they did when we were la

7.5 point
Here is another example of how human emotions can influence the course of events. Consider

8 point
Part of the problem of getting people to take cognitive mapping seriously is that it seems

8.5 point
A great deal can be learned about a company by looking at their personnel and the p

9 point
The start of any innovative process must be the willingness to take risks at the e

9.5 point
How each man handles fear varies with his personality. I take to my bunk and

10 point
Just before the curtain falls, the Corry, our sister ship, is rocked by a hug

10.5 point
Anyone looking back is likely to recall the brief, euphoric afterglow o

11 point
Young Henri displayed a talent for sketching, and an acquaintance

11.5 point
For young Americans of the day, study abroad was essential. Pa

12 point
After we reached that conclusion we started doing things righ

14 point
Even when clear objectives exist they are often not m

16 point
She was remarkably beautiful, celebrated for h

18 point
Nothing is more exhilarating than shared

20 point
Palms decorate a desert oasis in Sout

24 point
We were standing on the edge o

30 point
Interestingly, this accumu

36 point
Even more significant

mm |10 |20 |30 |40 |50 |60 |70 |80 |90 |100 |110

7 point
7/7 This paragraph is an example of type set solid. The term solid refers to any typographic composition set without space added between two or more lines of type. In visual terms, solid text provides a uniform grey value that is esthetically pleasing but that becomes tiring to the eyes during sustained reading. However, the visual quality intended or mor

7/8 This paragraph is an example of type set with one point of leading. The term leading refers to the amount of space added between two or more lines of type. The choice of leading depends not only on the designer's intention but also on the type size, line length, characteristics of the typeface used, and the quantity of text, among other things. The i

7/9 This paragraph is an example of type set with two points of leading. By increasing the leading, even in one point increments, the lines of type, especially in smaller sizes, start to separate into individual bands. This may inhibit the flow of reading with easy transition from one line to the next. Ultimately, the visual quality intended by the designer and th

7.5 point
7.5/7.5 This paragraph is an example of type set solid. The term solid refers to any typographic composition set without space added between two or more lines of type. In visual terms, solid text provides a uniform grey value that is esthetically pleasing but that becomes tiring to the eyes during sustained reading. However, the visual qua

7.5/8.5 This paragraph is an example of type set with one point of leading. The term leading refers to the amount of space added between two or more lines of type. The choice of leading depends not only on the designer's intention but also on the type size, line length, characteristics of the typeface used, and the quantity of text, among

7.5/9.5 This paragraph is an example of type set with two points of leading. By increasing the leading, even in one point increments, the lines of type, especially in smaller sizes, start to separate into individual bands. This may inhibit the flow of reading with easy transition from one line to the next. Ultimately, the visual quality intended

8 point
8/8 This paragraph is an example of type set solid. The term solid refers to any typographic composition set without space added between two or more lines of type. In visual terms, solid text provides a uniform grey value that is esthetically pleasing but that becomes tiring to the eyes during sustained reading. However, the visual quality intended or more pr

8/9 This paragraph is an example of type set with one point of leading. The term leading refers to the amount of space added between two or more lines of type. The choice of leading depends not only on the designer's intention but also on the type size, line length, characteristics of the typeface used, and the quantity of text, among other things. The introd

8/10 This paragraph is an example of type set with two points of leading. By increasing the leading, even in one point increments, the lines of type, especially in smaller sizes, start to separate into individual bands. This may inhibit the flow of reading with easy transition from one line to the next. Ultimately, the visual quality intended by the designer and the sp

Y

i

This logotype for an
architectural firm is based
on the contrast between
bold and light. A linear,
light triangle behind the
bold Y implies a capital A,
the negative white square
in the center alludes
to the letter i (for Inc.).

Contrast is vital to the design of
symbols and logotypes. A good
symbol is characterized by strong
contrasts both within itself and
with its surrounding elements.
A symbol must make a clear visual
statement that can be instantly
recalled: its design must be strong,
memorable, and enduring.
Letterforms and geometric elements
are ideal basic components for
the design of logotypes and
symbols. They are sophisticated,
ready-made elements which often
need only minimal refinement.

*In this logotype for a
gasoline distributor, the
capital M is modified
to resemble a traffic sign.*

*This logotype for a
publishing firm is based
on the contrast between an
angular and a curvilinear
form. The rhomboid
with the white letter S
evokes a third dimension.*

*This logotype for an
international industrial
conglomerate is based on
the contrast between
the oval inner counterform
and the angular outer
form. The counterform
of the letter G becomes
the focal point.*

*This logotype for a group
of furniture designers
is based on the contrast
of a two and a three
dimensional letter D. The
juxtaposition suggests
a lounge chair*

*This logotype for an
office park is based on the
contrast between a
curvilinear and an angular
form. The angle of the
letter K pointing into
the oval C evokes the enclo-
sure of the built space.*

Form and counterform

The most fundamental aspect of typographic design is the interplay between letterform and background. Against its background, every letterform defines a particular counterform. Form and counterform are interdependent, reciprocal values, each integral to a letter's design. The counterform is not simply the reversal of form: it is a new entity, the part of the background that emerges through interaction with the form.

When combined, letterforms create new counterforms between them. Tight spacing intensifies the counterforms between letters, while open spacing emphasizes those in the individual letter. The counterforms created by varying line lengths, make ragged right composition visually lighter and more playful than justified type.

Typographic design depends on the synergy of form and counterform. Elements must be arranged so that counterforms are clearly defined. The qualities of the background – its size and shape – are vital for the expression of any design. In judging design, evaluations must consider not only form but also counterform.

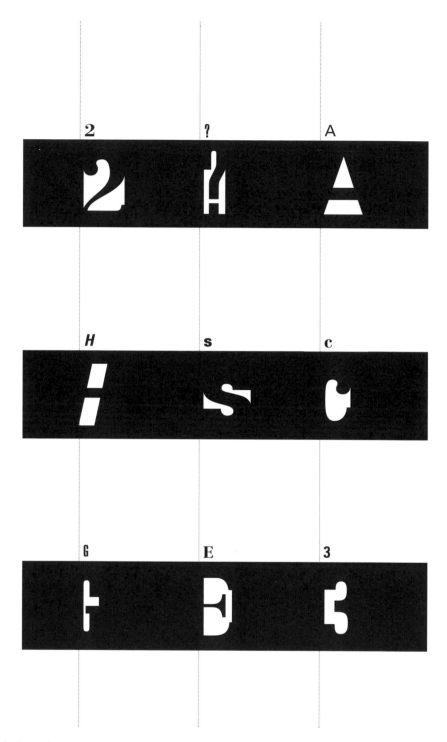

Against its background, every letterform defines a particular counterform. This counterform is a distinct and important part of the composition.

In the counterforms of letters there exists a fascinating new world of forms. Some counterforms are clear and simple, immediately revealing the character of a particular letter, while others are ambiguous or mysterious.

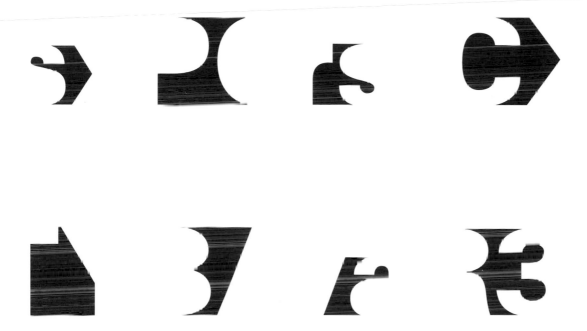

When letterforms are
combined, new counter-
forms emerge between
them. The background now
becomes the form, as
the letter's original form
submerges. The counter-
forms between letters are
a rich vocabulary of new
visual signs that are
ultimately determined by
the structure of language
and grammar.

Interesting graphic
solutions for logotypes can
often be discovered
through experimentation
with form and counterform.

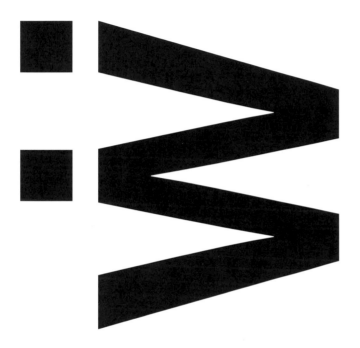

Letterform combinations from a class in introductory typography at Ohio State University. Through free experimentation with upper case letters, numerals, and punctuation marks composed in 72 point Helvetica Medium, the students gradually became familiar with the idiosyncrasies of typographic elements – their forms, counterforms, and micro-aesthetic details – and furthered their awareness of how to combine common typographic elements to create new signs.

THE
new

TIME SENSE OF

TYPOGRAPHIC

man

is

cinematic

sequential

pictorial

1

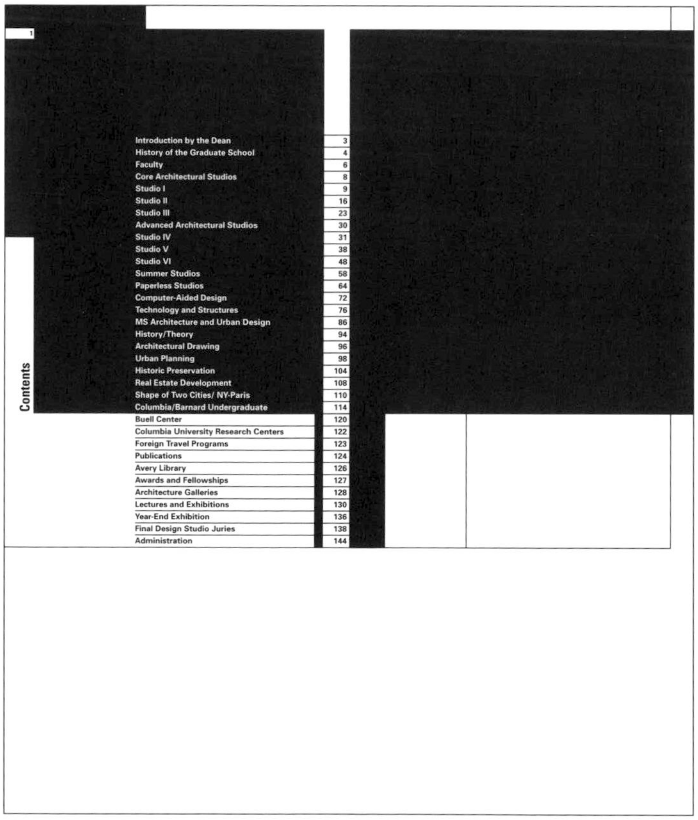

Contents

2

In designing the examples on this page, equal importance was given to form and counterform.

1 The form of this quote by Marshall McLuhan was developed to suggest motion and space. The form evokes an equally interesting counterform. 11.75 x 12.5 in

2 Two black rectangles create an intense, vertical counterform that high-lights the page numbers in this table of contents. 8.5 x 10 in

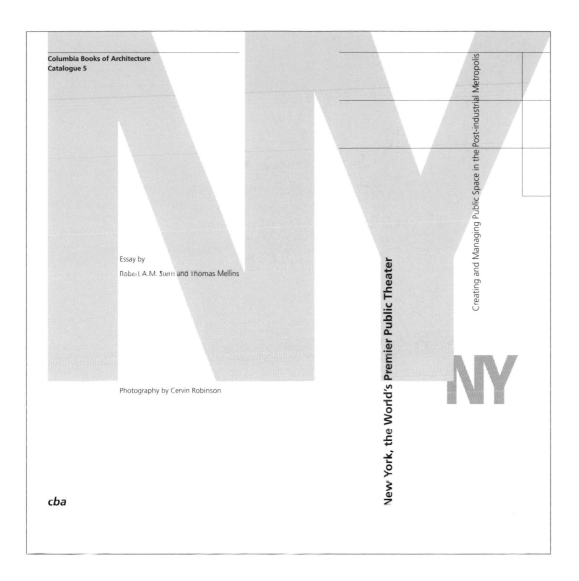

Columbia Books of Architecture
Catalogue 5

Essay by
Robert A.M. Stern and Thomas Mellins

Photography by Cervin Robinson

cba

New York, the World's Premier Public Theater

Creating and Managing Public Space in the Post-industrial Metropolis

NY

*The forms and counter-
forms of the letters
NY provide the structure
for the arrangement of
text on this title page of
an exhibition catalog.
The position of the lines
of type is determined
by the forms and counter-
forms of the letters NY.
The edges of the letter-
forms subdivide
lines of type between
individual words.
9x9 in*

3

Macro- and microaesthetics

In addition to sending objective messages (effect), typographic design inevitably expresses subjective emotions (affect). Effect communicates what is cognized, affect how it is perceived.

Typographic design is realized on two aesthetic scales: macro (explicit and obvious) and micro (subtle, sophisticated, perhaps only subconsciously perceptible). While both effect and affect occur at either scale, the former predominates in macroaesthetics, the latter in micro- aesthetics. Macroaesthetics comprise the most basic aspects of typographic design: overall format, dominant type, basic structure, color. Macroaesthetics are obvious, a single glance suffices to take them in.

Microaesthetics, however, demand a second look, or even deeper study, to be fully appreciated, to bring to conscious awareness the variety of details and compositional complexities. Not only do microaesthetics solve a specific communi- cation problem: equally, they reveal the aesthetic sensibilities and creative intelligence of the designer.

Typographic design can only be creatively and meaning-
fully practiced once we recognize that design communicates on two interrelated levels: macroaesthetic and
microaesthetic.

At the macroaesthetic level, the primary visual components
of a design are recognized first: size and proportion
of space; form, composition, and color of key elements;
the structure as a whole; and contrast between the
primary components and the space around them. Macroaesthetics capture the readers' initial attention and
lead them to the more complex microaesthetic level.

Microaesthetics encompass the form, size, weight, and
relationship of secondary elements: typeface characteristics; letterforms and counterforms; and spacing between letters, words, lines, and other graphic elements.
Although macroaesthetics may initially seem more
important, microaesthetics play the most significant role
in the quality and expression of a visual composition.
A design which does not work on the microaesthetic level
will often fail as an effective means of communication.

A design, whether simple or complex, must be viewed
as a combination of unique, interrelated microaesthetic
compositions. Though these compositions may to
some extent be determined by the grammatical
structure and sequence of language, it is ultimately the
designer who selects and controls the arrangement
of the elements.

The macro- and microaesthetic levels balance each other
in a design. A simple message may be enhanced by a visually challenging macroarrangement of elements,
while a highly structured and complex set of information
may benefit from a microaesthetically simple solution.

Through the conscious and objective use of the macro- and
microaesthetic dimensions, it is possible to devise a visual
vocabulary and design methodology, a set of principles,
which can be used in solving any design problem.
To the designer with a keen interest in typography, microaesthetics offer a rich and largely untapped source
of creative and intelligent solutions. In developing new
design directions, designers are challenged to build
and expand on the basic microaesthetic qualities inherent
in typography.

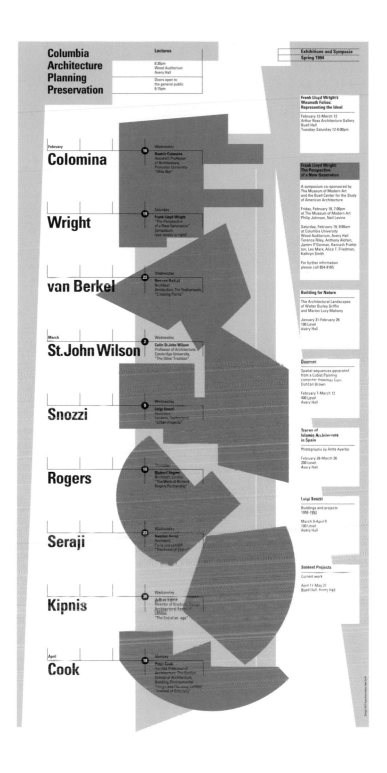

Lectures

6:30pm
Wood Auditorium
Avery Hall

Doors open to
the general public
6:15pm

Exhibitions and Symposia
Spring 1994

Frank Lloyd Wright's
Wasmuth Folios:
Representing the Ideal

February 12-March 12
Arthur Ross Architecture Gallery
Buell Hall
Tuesday-Saturday 12-6:00pm

February

Wednesday
16

Colomina

Beatriz Colomina
Assistant Professor
of Architecture,
Princeton University
"Mies Not"

Frank Lloyd Wright:
The Perspective
of a New Generation

A symposium co-sponsored by
The Museum of Modern Art
and the Buell Center for the Study
of American Architecture

Friday, February 18, 7:00pm
at The Museum of Modern Art
Philip Johnson, Neil Levine

Saturday, February 19, 9:00am
at Columbia University
Wood Auditorium, Avery Hall
Terence Riley, Anthony Alofsin,
James O'Gorman, Kenneth Framp-
ton, Leo Marx, Alice T. Friedman,
Kathryn Smith

For further information
please call 854-8165

Saturday
18

Wright

Frank Lloyd Wright
"The Perspective
of a New Generation"
Symposium
(see details at right)

Wednesday
23

van Berkel

Ben van Berkel
Architect
Amsterdam, The Netherlands
"Crossing Points"

Building for Nature

The Architectural Landscapes
of Walter Burley Griffin
and Marion Lucy Mahony

January 31-February 26
100 Level
Avery Hall

March

Wednesday
2

St.John Wilson

Colin St.John Wilson
Professor of Architecture,
Cambridge University,
"The Other Tradition"

Overview

Spatial sequences generated
from a Cubist Painting
computer drawings from
Duncan Brown

February 7-March 12
400 Level
Avery Hall

Wednesday
9

Snozzi

Luigi Snozzi
Architect
Locarno, Switzerland
"Urban Projects"

Traces of
Islamic Architecture
in Spain

Photographs by Anita Ayerbe

February 28-March 26
200 Level
Avery Hall

Thursday
10

Rogers

Richard Rogers
Architect, London
"The Work of Richard
Rogers Partnership"

Luigi Snozzi

Buildings and projects
1958-1992

March 9-April 9
100 Level
Avery Hall

Wednesday
23

Seraji

Nasrine Seraji
Architect,
Paris and Vienna
"Development of Space"

Student Projects

Current work

April 11-May 21
Buell Hall, Avery Hall

Wednesday
30

Kipnis

Jeffrey Kipnis
Director of Graduate Design
Architectural Association
"The End of an Age"

April

Monday
18

Cook

Peter Cook
Harried Professor of
Architecture, The Bartlett
School of Architecture,
Building, Environmental
Design and Planning, London
"Instead of Ordinary"

"2 x 24 in

All typographic design can be viewed as an assemblage of different layers of visual information. Each layer contributes to the macro- or the microaesthetic communication and is integral to the overall design. The layers of visual information are interdependent; they must be developed simultaneously. Various visual layers may be introduced for aesthetic or functional purposes such as attracting attention or establishing a hierarchy of information. Interesting visual layering may result from the spatial proximity of typographic elements. Through minimal changes in type size and weight, visual layers can be created. Some elements protrude to the foreground while others recede into the background, establishing a visual hierarchy that is essential to all typographic communication.

Poster for a series of lectures and exhibitions at Columbia University Graduate School of Architecture, Planning, and Preservation, New York.

The three layers of visual information from the poster on page 99. Each layer also functions as a single visual entity.

Foreground. The composition of six geometric shapes to attract attention. The shapes allude to the architectural theme of the lectures and exhibitions, and are arranged to create the illusion of motion and depth. The image communicates at the macroaesthetic level and contributes significantly to the character of the poster.

Middleground. The typographic information to announce the nine lectures and exhibitions. Its tight structure is in strong contrast to the free visual arrangement of geometric shapes. This layer of information is based on a square grid that has its own microaesthetic qualities.

Background. The geometric planes to support the typographic information and to connect the foreground and the middleground. During the design process, the configuration of these background shapes was repeatedly modified to accommodate changes in typographic information.

Poster announcing an exhibition of photographs. The juxtaposition of photographs is based on syntactic and semantic considerations – large, small; famous man (Marcello Mastroianni), anonymous woman. Designed in 1978, the poster has been labeled by design critics "a quintessential example of New Wave design."

Fredrich **Cantor**

strange *VICISSITUDES*

June 17
July 8
78

FOTO
492 Broome Street
New York, NY 10013

20 x 16 in

Dot pattern alludes to the lights in the large photograph.
Block of large, horizontal type contrasts with small type in the vertical white band.
Block composition of date anchors type to the edge of the poster.
Diagonal title contrasts with the counter-diagonal arrangement of the two photographs.

The computer is an excellent tool for exploring and refining the macro- and microaesthetics of typographic design. A document can be set up so that each layer can be viewed separately.

The technical possibility of creating so many visual layers, though, sometimes obscures the question of how many layers are appropriate. In an optimum solution, each visual layer should be effective on its own.

Fredrich Cantor

strange VICISSITUDES

1

1 The macroaesthetic
components.
2 The microaesthetic
components.
In many instances, the
design elements cannot
be separated clearly.
Some elements can
arguably belong to either
the macro- or the
microaesthetic level.

2

FOTO
492 Broome Street
New York, NY 10013

Mastroianni on Hudson Street, retitled Saul of Tarsus on the Road to Damascus

Fredrich
Cantor

June 17
July   8
78

Saul of Tarsus on the Road to Damascus

F

F
C

8
78

*Details from the poster
on page 102. Contrast and
identity of elements at
the microaesthetic level.*

Contrasts

horizontal:vertical
large:small
regular:bold

large:small
angular:linear

angular:round
regular:bold

Contrasts

flush left:flush right

light:bold

positive:negative
regular:bold

strange **V I C I S S I T U D E S**

strange **V I C**

Contrasts

small:large
short:long

light:bold
close:open

direction of strokes

Identities

dot texture

dot composition

dot

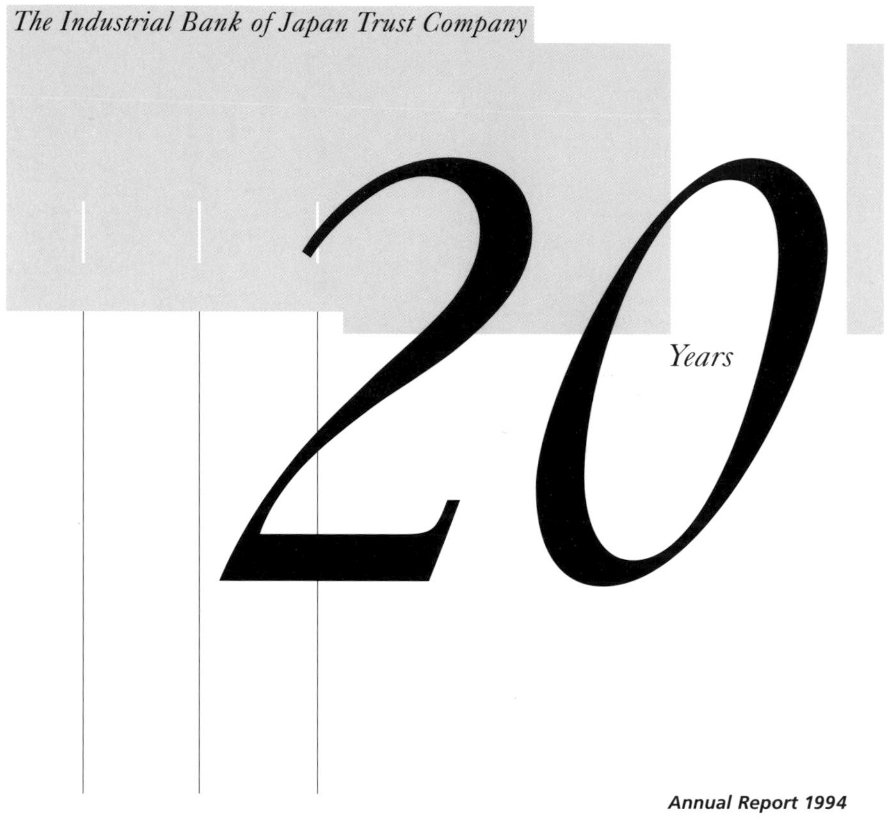

The Industrial Bank of Japan Trust Company

20

Years

8.25 x 11.75 in

Annual Report 1994

**Cover design for the
Industrial Bank
of Japan Trust Company
20th anniversary
annual report.**

**In the orthogonal
design the large italic
numerals suggest
dynamic motion and
progress.**

The Industrial Bank of Japan Trust Company

Years

Annual Report 1994

Years

1	2
3	4
5	

1 The large dynamic numerals in the foreground contrast with the static rectangular field in the background.
2 The typography corresponds with the vertical white space in the grey field.
3 The curvilinear numeral contrasts with the vertical lines.

4 The large zero draws attention to Years.
5 The short bold lines contrast with the long fine lines. The two colums refer to the columns in the financial statements.

UNITY

Anspach
Grossman
Portugal
Inc

6 x 6 in

1972

*Season's greetings
card for Anspach Grossman
Portugal Inc.
Circular microaesthetic
details, extracted from the
word UNITY, are printed on
two squares of clear
acetate. The remaining
parts of the letters and the
company name are printed
on white Kromekote.*

*The three pieces were
inserted in random order
into the envelope before
mailing. By assembling
the pieces in the proper
sequence the recipient was
able to create UNITY.*

Anspach
Grossman
Portugal
Inc

1972

72

Anspach
Grossman
Portugal
Inc

1 72

1

Anspach
Grossman
Portugal
Inc

972

1	2
3	4
5	6

*Circular shapes high-
light the microaesthetic
details of form and
counterform for the five
letters in UNITY.
1 Fragments of UNITY
are printed on Kromekote.
3 5 Circular shapes are
printed on clear acetate.
2 4 6 The three layers are
assembled to form
various permutations of
the card.*

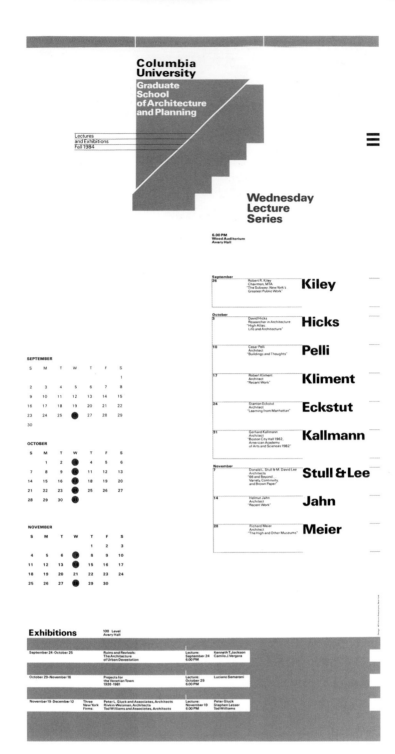

Columbia University
Graduate School of Architecture and Planning

Lectures
and Exhibitions
Fall 1984

Wednesday Lecture Series

6.00 PM
Wood Auditorium
Avery Hall

September 26	Robert R. Kiley Chairman, MTA "The Subway: New York's Greatest Public Work"	**Kiley**
October 3	David Hicks Researcher in Architecture "High Atlas: Life and Architecture"	**Hicks**
10	Cesar Pelli Architect "Buildings and Thoughts"	**Pelli**
17	Robert Kliment Architect "Recent Work"	**Kliment**
24	Stanton Eckstut Architect "Learning from Manhattan"	**Eckstut**
31	Gerhard Kallmann Architect "Boston City Hall 1962, American Academy of Arts and Sciences 1982"	**Kallmann**
November 7	Donald L. Stull & M. David Lee Architects "66 and Beyond... Variety, Continuity, and Brown Paper"	**Stull & Lee**
14	Helmut Jahn Architect "Recent Work"	**Jahn**
28	Richard Meier Architect "The High and Other Museums"	**Meier**

SEPTEMBER

S	M	T	W	T	F	S
						1
2	3	4	5	6	7	8
9	10	11	12	13	14	15
16	17	18	19	20	21	22
23	24	25	●	27	28	29
30						

OCTOBER

S	M	T	W	T	F	S
	1	2	●	4	5	6
7	8	9	●	11	12	13
14	15	16	●	18	19	20
21	22	23	●	25	26	27
28	29	30	●			

NOVEMBER

S	M	T	W	T	F	S
				1	2	3
4	5	6	●	8	9	10
11	12	13	●	15	16	17
18	19	20	21	22	23	24
25	26	27	●	29	30	

12 x 24 in

Exhibitions 100 Level
Avery Hall

September 24–October 25	Ruins and Revivals: The Architecture of Urban Devastation	Lecture: September 24 6.00 PM	Kenneth T. Jackson Camilo J. Vergara
October 29–November 16	Projects for the Venetian Town 1926–1981	Lecture: October 29 6.00 PM	Luciano Semerani
November 19–December 12	Three New York Firms:	Peter L. Gluck and Associates, Architects Rivkin-Weisman, Architects Tod Williams and Associates, Architects	Lecture: November 19 6.00 PM	Peter Gluck Stephen Lesser Tod Williams

Poster announcing a series of nine lectures and three exhibitions held over a three-month period at the Columbia University Graduate School of Architecture, Planning and Preservation.

The geometric shape at the top, cut diagonally into two contrasting forms, alludes to the architectural themes of the lectures and serves as the regulating structure for the typography below. Lecture and exhibition dates are highlighted on the calendar.

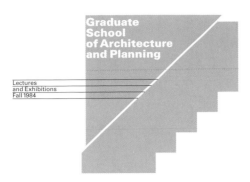

**Graduate
School
of Architecture
and Planning**

Lectures
and Exhibitions
Fall 1984

S	M	T	W	T	F	S
9	10	11	12	13	14	15
16	17	18	19	20	21	22
23	24	25	(26)	27	28	29
30						

OCTOBER

S	M	T	W	T	F	S
	1	2	(3)	4	5	6
7	8	9	(10)	11	12	13
14	15	16	(17)	18	19	20
21	22	23	(24)	25	26	27
28	29	30	(31)			

NOVEMBER

S	M	T	W	T	F	S
				1	2	3
4	5	6	(7)	8	9	10
11	12	13	(14)	15	16	17
18	19	20	21	22	23	24
25	26	27	(28)	29	30	

**Wednesday
Lecture
Series**

6.00 PM
Wood Auditorium
Avery Hall

September
26   Robert R. Kiley
Chairman, MTA
"The Subway: New York's
Greatest Public Work"

Kiley

October
3   David Hicks
Researcher in Architecture
"High Atlas:
Life and Architecture"

Hicks

10   Cesar Pelli
Architect
"Buildings and Thoughts"

Pelli

17   Robert Kliment
Architect
"Recent Work"

Kliment

24   Stanton Eckstut
Architect
"Learning from Manhattan"

Eckstut

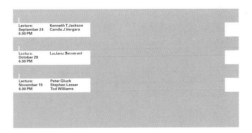

Lecture:	Kenneth T.Jackson
September 24	Camilo J.Vergara
6.00 PM	

Lecture:	Luciano Semerani
October 29	
6.00 PM	

Lecture:	Peter Gluck
November 19	Stephen Lesser
6.00 PM	Tod Williams

1	2
3	4
5	

1 Horizontal lines,
penetrating the diagonally
cut surface, create an
illusion of depth.
2 Three type weights
differentiate individual
months, and suggest a
progression of time.
3 The regulating structure
for the typography is
provided by the stepped
form in the square.

4 The line structure
coordinates the lecture
date, title, and lecturer's
name.
5 Horizontal light and
dark bands allude to
exhibition spaces located
below ground level.

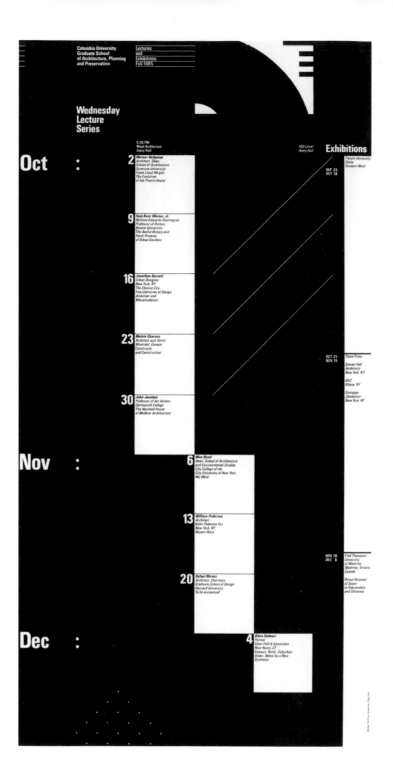

12 x 24 in

Poster announcing a series of nine lectures and three exhibitions held over a three-month period at the Columbia University Graduate School of Architecture, Planning and Preservation.

Five lectures were given in October, three in November, and one in December. This 5:3:1 ratio determined the macro-aesthetic structure, consisting of nine squares stepping from top left to bottom right.

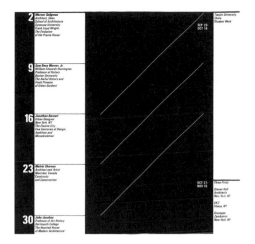

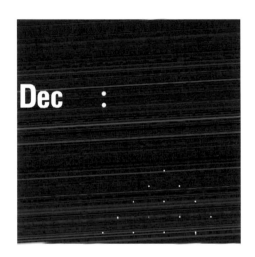

Columbia University Graduate School of Architecture, Planning and Preservation Lectures and Exhibitions Fall 1985

Wednesday Lecture Series

6.00 PM
Wood Auditorium
Avery Hall

1	2
3	4
5	

1 Diagonal lines connect lectures with concurrent exhibitions.
2 An abstract design element alludes to the architectural theme of the lectures.
3 The arrangement of squares in steps from left to right suggests the progression of time.
4 The dot pattern echoes the graphic theme of squares.

5 The structure of the typography is determined by the macrostructure of the poster.

12 x 24 in

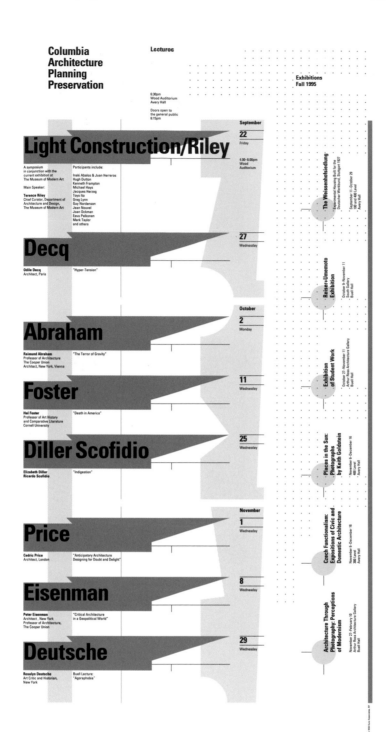

**Columbia
Architecture
Planning
Preservation**

Lectures

6:30pm
Wood Auditorium
Avery Hall

Doors open to
the general public
6:15pm

**Exhibitions
Fall 1995**

September
22
Friday

Light Construction/Riley

A symposium
in conjunction with the
current exhibition at
The Museum of Modern Art

Main Speaker:

Terence Riley
Chief Curator, Department of
Architecture and Design,
The Museum of Modern Art

Participants include:

Iñaki Abalos & Juan Herreros
Hugh Dutton
Kenneth Frampton
Michael Hays
Jacques Herzog
Toyo Ito
Greg Lynn
Guy Nordenson
Jean Nouvel
Joan Ockman
Eeva Pelkonen
Mark Taylor
and others

4:00–8:00pm
Wood
Auditorium

The Weissenhofsiedlung
Experimental Housing Built for the
Deutscher Werkbund, Stuttgart 1927

September 11–October 29
300 and 400 Level
Avery Hall

Decq

Odile Decq
Architect, Paris

"Hyper-Tension"

27
Wednesday

**Reiser+Umemoto
Exhibition**

October 9–November 11
South Gallery
Buell Hall

October
2
Monday

Abraham

Raimund Abraham
Professor of Architecture
The Cooper Union
Architect, New York, Vienna

"The Terror of Gravity"

**Exhibition
of Student Work**

October 27–November 11
Arthur Ross Architecture Gallery
Buell Hall

11
Wednesday

Foster

Hal Foster
Professor of Art History
and Comparative Literature
Cornell University

"Death in America"

**Places in the Sun:
Photographs
by Keith Goldstein**

November 6–December 16
400 Level
Avery Hall

25
Wednesday

Diller Scofidio

**Elizabeth Diller
Ricardo Scofidio**

"Indigestion"

November
1
Wednesday

Price

Cedric Price
Architect, London

"Anticipatory Architecture
Designing for Doubt and Delight"

**Czech Functionalism:
Expositions of Civic and
Domestic Architecture**

November 6–December 16
300 Level
Avery Hall

8
Wednesday

Eisenman

Peter Eisenman
Architect , New York
Professor of Architecture,
The Cooper Union

"Critical Architecture
in a Geopolitical World"

**Architecture Through
Photography: Perceptions
of Modernism**

November 27–February 18
Arthur Ross Architecture Gallery
Buell Hall

29
Wednesday

Deutsche

Rosalyn Deutsche
Art Critic and Historian,
New York

Buell Lecture:
"Agoraphobia"

*Poster announcing a
series of eight lectures and
six exhibitions held over
a three-month period at the
Columbia University
Graduate School of
Architecture, Planning and
Preservation.*

*Eight sharp geometric
shapes, protruding into the
format from the left,
point to the lecture dates.
Three free-form geo-
metric shapes, one for each
month, subdivide the
format vertically into two
areas: lectures on the
left, exhibitions on the right.*

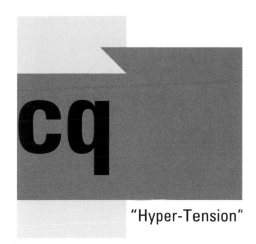

"Hyper-Tension"

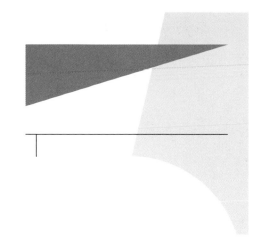

25
Wednesday

8
Wednesday

Reiser-
Exhibit

1	2
3	4
5	

1 A sharp triangular cut
in the band directs the eye
to the lecture title.
2 3 4 Irregular edges
create different configura-
tions between the
geometric shapes and
the arrows.
5 The vertical placement
of the exhibition listings
contrasts with the horizontal placement of the
lectures. Each of the six
exhibition titles is

anchored to a large
circle which contrasts with
the small dots of the background pattern.

4.125 x 5.75 in

**400 Level Gallery, Avery Hall
Columbia University
Graduate School of Architecture
Planning and Preservation**

Willi Kunz

April 17
May 5

Architectural
Typography II

Arch
Typo

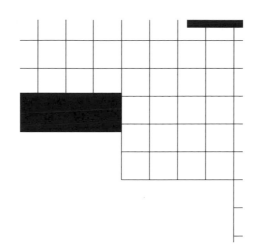

April 17
May 5

1	2
3	4
5	

1 Vertical and horizontal
lines highlight the first
part of each word,
combining them visually
into the new expression
ArchTypo.

2 A square grid deter-
mines the size and compo-
sition of typographic
elements.

3 Forced block compo-
sition of exhibition dates
conforms to orthogonal
design of the card.

4 The white circle
contrasts with the black
triangular form of the
letter A.

5 A dynamic diagonal
contrasts with the compo-
sition of static squares.

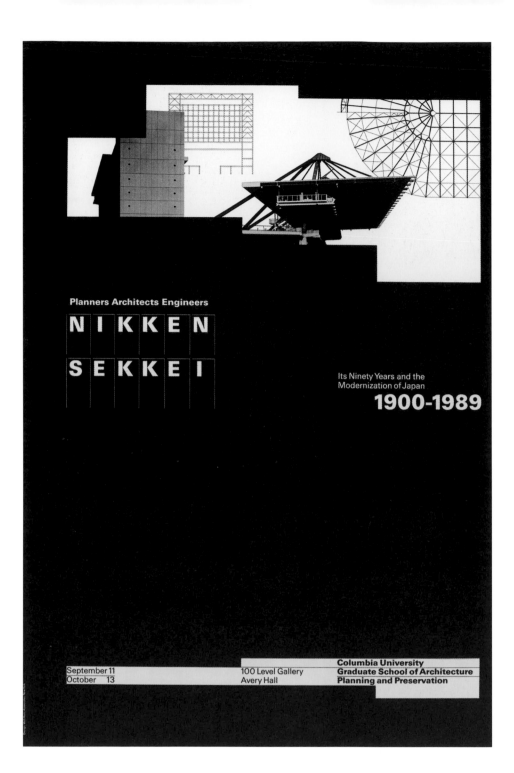

Planners Architects Engineers

NIKKEN
SEKKEI

Its Ninety Years and the
Modernization of Japan

1900-1989

18×27 in

September 11	100 Level Gallery	**Columbia University**
October 13	Avery Hall	**Graduate School of Architecture**
		Planning and Preservation

*Poster for a traveling
exhibition of work
by Nikken Sekkei, Japan's
largest planning, archi-
tecture and engineering
firm.*

*The photographs and
drawings in the stepped
window were chosen
for their contrasting visual
qualities. The window
concept relates to the
firm's 90th anniversary,
and metaphorically
expresses a simultaneous
glance into the past and
the future.*

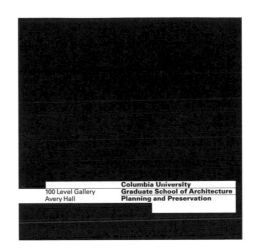

Columbia University
Graduate School of Architecture
100 Level Gallery **Planning and Preservation**
Avery Hall

Planners Architects Engineers

NIKKEN
SEKKEI

Its Ninety Years and the
Modernization of Japan
1900-1989

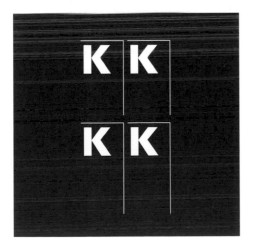

1	2
3	4
5	

1 *The stepped window
coordinates the four
dissimilar visual images.*
2 *The composition of
gallery information makes
visual reference to the
large window.*
3 5 *The repeated sequence
of letterforms in the
two words determines the
typographic composition.*

4 *The static blocks of
type are shifted horizon-
tally to emphasize
the anniversary dates.*

18 x 24 in

Recruitment poster for Columbia University's one-year undergraduate study program in architecture, urban planning, and historic preservation held in New York and Paris.

The primary visual elements are a circle representing the world, and six photographs of urban landscapes typical of New York and Paris. The vertical and horizontal shapes of the photographs reflect the predominant building forms of each of the two cities.

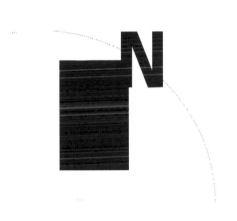

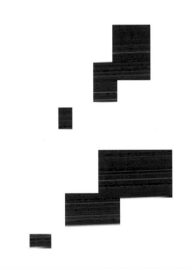

1 At the macroaesthetic level, a large circle with two dots represents Paris and New York as positioned on the globe.
2 The dots for "New York" and "Paris" visually establish a connection between the two cities.
3 The picture shape makes reference to the shape of the N.

4 The gradations in size of the photographs convey distance.
5 "New York" is anchored to the frame by the negative space corresponding to the letter K.

Bernard Tschumi
Dean

Columbia University
Graduate School of Architecture,
Planning, and Preservation

requests the pleasure
of your company for the
opening of

at
Columbia
University
Architecture
Galleries

4.25 x 6 in

May 11–31

Saturday,	Buell Hall and
May 11	Avery Hall
6:00 – 8:00pm	100
reception	400
and viewing	500

Invitation for an exhibition of student projects in architecture, urban planning and historic preservation at Columbia University.

The central composition of divergent yet carefully structured elements suggests the experimental character of the work exhibited. The exhibition title seems to float behind the three transparent slanted rectangles.

M

N^R

H

-OF-
iTi

●

1	2
3	4
5	6

1 "Exhibit" is highlighted through placement against two solid rectangles.
2 The active, rectangular letter M in the foreground contrasts with the passive circle in the background.
3 The diminished type size of the upper line is determined by the relationship of the R to the vertical stroke of the N.

4 The line elements overlapping the slanted letter H at a contrasting angle evoke the impression of space.
5 Through coordinated letter spacing the hyphens become dots for the I's in the lower line.
6 The size of the round dot corresponds to the space between the line elements.

DESIGN
594 B

Advanced **T**ypography

An experimental workshop
with typographic materials
and their use in relation to
color, illustration, photography and structure.
Emphasizes individual exploration of areas of
particular interest.

Knowledge in Basic Typography is a prerequisite for this course

13.75 x 16.5 in

For further information and permission to register call 422 8102
Department of Industrial Design, OSU, 374 Hopkins Hall, 128 North Oval Drive

*Poster announcing an
experimental workshop in
advanced typography
at Ohio State University.
The graphic composition
with the letter T was
cut in linoleum and printed
together with the rest
of the type in letterpress.*

T

DESIGN
594   B

DESIGN
594   B

T

Knowledge in Basic Typography is a prerequisite for this course

DESIGN
594   B

Advanced **T**ypography

An experimental workshop
with typographic materials
and their use in relation to
color, illustration, photography and structure.
Emphasizes individual exploration of areas of
particular interest.

1	2
3	4
5	

1 The initial design
elements: three capital T's
of different sizes.
2 Changes of letterform
scale, rotation, and
combination with two
negative T's determined
the composition.
3 The justified composition
of the course number
refers the horizontal stroke
of the T.

4 The long line of type
contrasts with the justified
composition of the course
number.
5 The visual structure
of the typography is based
on the angular composition
of the letterform T.

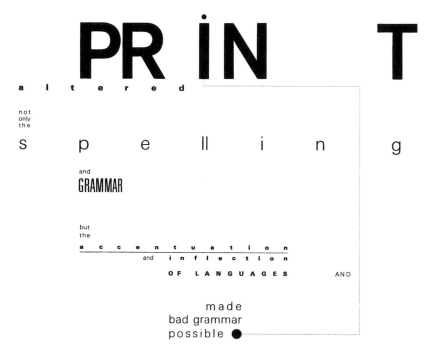

11.75 x 12.5 in

PR IN T
altered
not
only
the
s p e ll i n g
and
GRAMMAR
but
the
a c c e n t u a t i o n
and i n f l e c t i o n
OF LANGUAGES   AND
m a d e
bad grammar
possible ●

Typographic interpretation of a quote by Marshall McLuhan from a series of studies in visual syntax and semantics.

*Through deliberate use of type style, size, and spacing, sections of the sentence are stressed, and the semantics of individual words underscored.
A strongly demarcated visual structure unifies the composition of divergent typographic elements.*

PR IN T

made
bad grammar
possible ●

s p e l l i n g

and
GRAMMAR

ll

g

i n f l e c t i o n
OF LANGUAGES   AND

made
bad grammar
possible ●

1 The angular line connects two key components of the sentence, creating a new sentence.
2 Extreme letter spacing reinforces the semantics of "spelling" – atomistic and individual; the extremely condensed typeface of "grammar" shows it semantically as rigid and unchangeable.

3 The typographic elements are structured for contrast between one heavy and two light verticals.
4 The bold angular T and the light oval g are placed for contrast. The angular line echoes the T.
5 Contrast in form and structure between two justified compositions.

1	2
3	4
5	

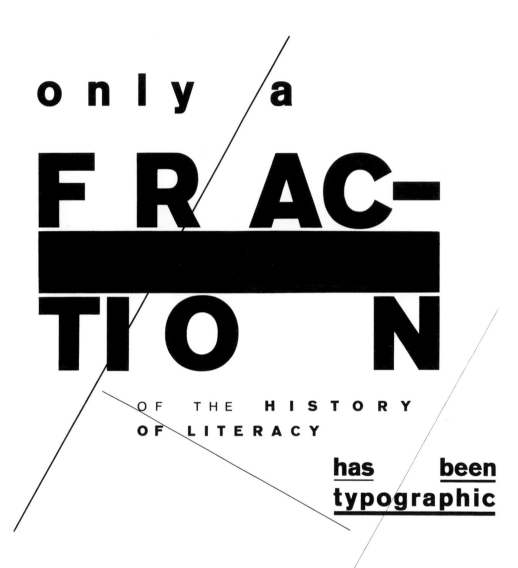

11.75x12.5 in

only a FRAC-TION OF THE HISTORY OF LITERACY has been typographic

Typographic interpretation of a quote by Marshall McLuhan from a series of studies in visual syntax and semantics.

"Fraction" is broken apart by the horizontal band and extreme irregular letter-spacing, and is thus given a semantic interpretation. Line elements are structured to intersect and divide words. Through variation in type size, weight, and composition, the sentence is subdivided into fragments of communicative statements.

N

typographic

has   been
typographic

F R AC-
TIO N

1 A diagonal line splits
the word "typographic,"
reinforcing the semantics
of the sentence. The
line angle determines the
letterspacing.
2 The negative space in
the first line corresponds to
the width of the letter N.
3 The line composition
fractures the space of the
sentence.

4 The combination of
the letter C and the hyphen
forms an arrow pointing
to the left.
5 By dividing the word,
the horizontal band
makes clear the semantics
of "fraction".

Cover design for a special issue of Typografische Monatsblätter, *featuring the graphic design program of Sadlier educational publishers, New York.*

The selection and composition of typographic elements refer to the four divisions of the company: religion, mathematics, economics, and social science.

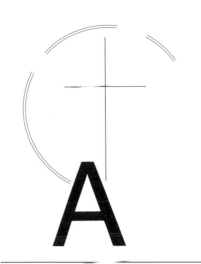

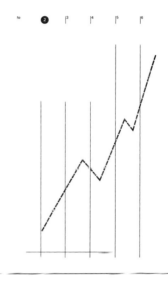

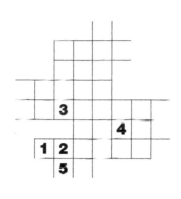

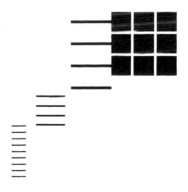

1 The letters ABC, diminishing in size and retreating in space, refer to different reading levels and school grades.
2 The sign of the Cross, merging with a triangular A, refers to the religious material published.
3 Economic growth is represented by bold, diagonal dashes intersecting a series of fine vertical rules.

4 Bold numerals within a grid suggest a mathematical problem. The irregular outer edge of the grid facilitates its integration with the surrounding elements.
5 Repetitions of line groupings, juxtaposed with a static composition of squares, evoke movement and space.

4

Synthesis

In typography, the first and most elusive step involves just one person – the designer – and the creation of a concept.

Highly influenced by the designer's visual sensibilities, this first step is taken on the macroaesthetic level. Later, smaller steps are taken on the microaesthetic level. Depending on the scope and scale of the project, later steps may take place at different times and places, and may involve other specialists with a variety of skills – photography, pre-press, printing, for instance.

Although designers need not be a master of all these skills, they must be aware of the requirements and limitations each specialist imposes on the project, as well as how, collectively, they contribute to the synergy required to develop and realize the original, conceptual idea. The process of typographic design is thus one of creating, refining, looping back, and synthesizing myriad demands and details; the product a synthesis of creative, administrative, and technical processes.

For every project, the purpose of the communication must be first established, and a conceptual framework created. With these in place, typographic principles and the nature of the information provide the basis from which to explore different visual approaches.

The difficulty is not only creating the concept but also in realizing it. This objective becomes increasingly elusive as the number of persons involved increases, each bringing his or her own objectives and biases to the problem. In evaluating designs, reasoning and judgment often become intertwined with emotion, making it difficult to reach consensus. A concept with an intellectual premise can make the process easier by offering a rationale that can be understood by everyone involved, including the intended audience. The argument for any design should be based on communication goals rather than aesthetics – which of course does not mean that aesthetics are unimportant.

Typographic principles lay the groundwork for any good design. All processes depend on a set of principles, rules, or guidelines in order to function. Traffic without laws is chaos; games cannot be played without rules. Typographic communication, as well, requires that certain basic grammatical and visual standards be followed, and that all parties share the same visual and verbal vocabulary.

Guidelines do not have to be stifling, however. Children playing games follow the rules with serious attention, but at the same time interpret them creatively. To work on a tightly defined problem is more challenging, and more exciting, than working on a problem without constraints. What initially appear to be constraints can also lead to unexpected solutions. For instance, a poster may be required to contain an unwieldy amount of disparate information, but this disparity might create an interesting visual structure.

When problems are too open-ended, the dazzling array of possibilities often leads to confused or chaotic results. A program, such as a grid system, a series of carefully selected type sizes and weights, or self-imposed technical or economic limitations helps channel the design process into a more productive and interesting course. The challenge is how to determine the best program for the particular situation: how much freedom, creativity, and intuition to allow. In many cases, this is determined by considerations of practicality, budget, and audience; the designer's level of experience; and whether the designer is working alone or as part of a team.

Useful as a program is, however, it alone cannot guarantee a successful outcome. Intelligence, talent, inspiration, and hard work are also necessary, as is a thorough understanding of the information to be represented. To allow for a coherent structure, the information must be carefully analyzed. The resulting hierarchy remains fixed, but lends itself to a variety of visual representations.

To realize the concept and meet the project's objectives, different visual approaches may be explored. This exploration gives shape to the macroaesthetics of the design, turning raw information into visual communication. Once a particular approach is chosen, further refinements take place at the microaesthetic level.

The final stages of the design process hone the aesthetic aspects. The microaesthetic level of a design can be continually refined and affords the greatest opportunity for improving the quality and expressiveness of a visual composition. The microaesthetic level also gives the designer a certain degree of freedom to go beyond resolving only the task at hand, to express his or her own sensibilities. Ideally, the combination of macro- and microaesthetic components forms a synthesis – a convincing design solution for a specific problem.

Every project is an interplay of a myriad of ideas, opinions, requirements, and economic and technical constraints. While it is often impossible to precisely identify all the factors that shape a solution, one thing is certain: a good concept is always vital.

After many years of working with the computer, I still find
pencil sketches the most efficient means of developing
conceptual studies. Rather than transcribing an idea
through the keyboard, computer, and printer, it seems
to me much more natural and direct to capture my
thoughts on a sheet of paper with a pencil. At the start of
a project it is extremely important to spend some
quality time focusing on objectives instead of getting
distracted by what the computer can or must do.

The computer, however, is invaluable once the project is
past the basic conceptual stage. Many design variations
can be developed and edited without the waste of
materials. Unintentional commands may lead to unexpected new directions. In realizing the original idea,
the macro- and microaesthetics can be infinitely refined
as the visual expression evolves to meet the objectives.
Whatever tools are used, a successful solution
must ultimately communicate its message and evoke
the desired emotional response.

*Selected sketches
for the poster on page 136.*

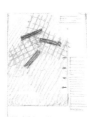

Poster announcing a symposium about the transformation of traditional public space into cyber-space and its deterioration into hyper-ghettos.

Purpose
To express the hyperactive, multilayered quality of today's urban environment, and to suggest the panelists' diverse points of view.

Macrostructure
The three symposium topics, with three layers of grids converging at different angles, provide visual depth.

Microaesthetics
Three layers of geometric planes of different size and shape, each gradated from light to dark, increase visual depth.

18 x 24 in

**Columbia University
Graduate School of Architecture
Planning and Preservation**

Master
of Science
in

and

Architecture | Urban Design

The Master of Science Degree in Architecture and Urban Design has been reformulated beginning in 1992-1993. It is an intensive three semester program for architects interested in post-professional specialization.

The curriculum is oriented toward the emerging urbanism in the United States, with a particular emphasis on the situation in New York City. It seeks to define parameters and problems which will carry into the next century. It also embraces a special relationship between the design studio and New York, through collaboration with city agencies and other public interest constituencies. Comparative study with other world cities is also considered central to the methods of discourse, focused on seminars and case studies.

The degree is intended to augment traditional professional training in architecture for those who wish to further investigate the physical aspects of urbanism. "Urban Design" is seen as an activist, social art more than a singular representation of physical scale; the term defines a commitment to discourse at all scales of design activity. In this sense, the unique situation of Columbia allows New York City to become a laboratory, in which the discipline of architecture can be applied to a myriad of problems within our urban environment at all scales of inquiry. At the same time, the more than rhetorical comparison of coursework allows for comparative study with other world cities and situations. The design studio is the primary catalyst for the curriculum, centered on a highly individualized, atelier approach.

The Columbia University Graduate School of Architecture, Planning and Preservation is a unique academic forum within which to pursue studies in Urban Design. The distinguished, nationally prominent faculty nurtures a wide-ranging critical perspective on the question of urbanism today. Classroom and studio teaching is reinforced by extensive lecture and publication programs. The Avery Architectural and Fine Arts Library is an invaluable resource, as the nation's finest repository for the literature of architecture, planning, and fine arts. In addition, the innumerable cultural resources of New York City, as a whole, are close at hand.

Bernard Tschumi, Dean   Richard Plunz, Director

Further information and application:
Columbia University
Office of Architecture Admissions
400 Avery Hall
New York, NY 10027
212/854-3414

Program

Emphasis

Resources

18 x 24 in

Poster announcing a
program in architecture and
urban design.

Purpose
To compare the fabric
and density of city, suburb
and industrial area.

Macrostructure
The stepped arrangement
and increasing size of
photographs suggest grad
ual expansion from city
to industrial environment.
The bold, irregular
frame defines the format
and anchors the text.

Microaesthetics
The line structure at the
top emphasizes the
two aspects of the program
and connects the program
title with the school name.
The line structure on the
left organizes the program
information.

Poster announcing two programs in architecture and urban design.

Purpose
To illustrate program content through examples of students' work.

Macrostructure
A triangular field, punctuated by three square photographs of building models, anchors the two program titles. The two triangles along the left-hand edge point to the program titles.

Microaesthetics
The typography at the top is based on a fourteen-column grid. The steps in the frame at the top differentiate the text elements. Negative text in the upper left-hand corner changes to positive text, providing a transition between the frame and the visual field. The architectural drawing in the background increases visual depth.

18 x 24 in

Columbia University
Graduate School of Architecture
Planning and Preservation

The expansion and revision of the Masters of Science Degree in Architecture and Building Design and Masters of Science Degree in Architecture and Urban Design are among several changes in the Graduate School of Architecture, Planning and Preservation which will sustain and deepen the excellence for which the School has been known since 1881. The following programs and projects, already in progress or planned for the 1989-1990 academic year, represent the new dynamics of the School.

Programs. To lend them greater coherence and intellectual rigor, the Urban Design and Building Design Programs have been expanded to three semesters with new courses and studios that integrate them with the resources of both the School and New York City.

Physical Facilities. To improve the School's historic Avery Hall (originally designed by McKim, Mead and White), extensive renovations are planned that will include the restoration of important spaces in the building and the air-conditioning of its studios. The adjacent Buell

Hall (location of the School's Temple Hoyne Buell Center for the Study of American Architecture) is now undergoing complete renovation that will provide the School with new classrooms and review and exhibition spaces.

Publications. To disseminate the critical and pedagogical intentions of its programs and studios, the School has initiated *Abstract,* an annual journal that is a public forum for the School's studio work. To encourage communication between the School and the larger design community, another new publication, *Newsline,* is a monthly journal of comment and news from the School. To enumerate the resources of New York City to the School's students, *Newsline* includes a complete listing of the city's exhibitions, lectures, and events concerning design. In addition, *Precis,* the publication series organized and edited by the School's students, will soon produce the book, *Architecture and Body,* to be published by Rizzoli.

Lectures and Events. To enhance its studios and academic offerings, the School sponsors an average of 15 special lectures by visitors and faculty each month. These lectures adjoin regularly scheduled exhibitions and symposia open to all students in the School. Recent guests include Raimund Abraham, Tadao Ando, Andrea Bosch, John Costonis, Peter Eisenman, Hal Foster, Zaha Hadid, Jan Henriksen, and Andreas Huyssen. Recent exhibitions and symposia include "New Schools in Catalonia," "Emerging European Architects," the works of Santiago Calatrava and "Robert Moses' New York." Planned events for the 1989-1990 academic year include exhibitions of the works of Giuseppe Terragni, the conferences "Currents in Contemporary Architectural Theory" and "Architects and Developers," and a School-wide charrette.

Faculty. Past and future faculty in the Building Design and Urban Design Programs include:

Neil Denari
Livia Dimitriu
Stanton Eckstut
Kenneth Frampton
Geoffrey Freeman
Romaldo Giurgola
Sigurd Grava
Miriam Gusevich
Zaha Hadid
Klaus Herdeg
Steven Holl
Andrea Kahn

Antonio Latini
Alessandra Latour
William MacDonald
Peter Marcuse
Sandro Marpillero
Mary McLeod
Michael Mein
Eric Owen Moss
Richard Plunz
James Stewart Polshek

Hani Rashid
Michael Rotundi
Saskia Sassen
Elliott Sclar
Robert A. M. Stern
Susana Torre
Bernard Tschumi
Antonio Velez-Catrain
Lauretta Vinciarelli
Rafael Viñoly
Harry Wolf
Gwendolyn Wright

The Graduate School of Architecture, Planning and Preservation stands at a historic moment in its development. New programs, facilities, publications and activities will provide the School's students with a unique opportunity to pursue design excellence.

Master of Science in Architecture and Building Design

Master of Science in Architecture and Urban Design

Master of Science in Advanced Architectural Design

Master of Science in Architecture and Urban Design

18 x 24 in

New design of the poster on page 138.

Purpose
To illustrate program content through examples of students' work.

Macrostructure
The photograph of an architectural model forms the core of the visual composition. The diagonally cut frame anchors the text and defines the background. The axonometric drawing creates visual depth.

Microaesthetics
The rectangular cut in the photograph emphasizes the placement of the program titles. The line structure at the top coordinates the program titles and school name. The change from positive to negative type at the top right facilitates the transition between frame and background.

Columbia University
Graduate School of Architecture
Planning and Preservation

Introduction to Architecture

A Summer Studio in New York

A summer program giving university credit which introduces the student to aspects of the design, history, theory, and practice of architecture. The program is intended both for those without previous academic experience in design who are interested in architecture as a potential career, and for those with previous experience in architectural design who would like to develop additional studio design skills, perhaps in preparation for application to graduate school.

Courses are given in the studios of Avery Hall, home of Columbia University's world-renowned Graduate School of Architecture, Planning, and Preservation, on the Morningside Heights campus in New York City. Studios and seminar courses are taught by experienced architects and designers, coordinated and supervised by members of the faculty of the Graduate School. For those who may require it, housing is available on the University campus, with direct access to Avery Hall.

Students attend classes four days a week for five weeks, both morning and afternoon sessions. In the morning session, students are introduced to the fundamentals of architectural history and theory, structures, technology, and professional practice. Also, this course will introduce the student to the extraordinary city of New York, with its world famous collection of museums, cultural institutions, and architectural monuments. Lectures, seminar presentations, tours of architect's offices, and field-trips to active building sites, museums, and famous works of architecture in New York City are led by the instructors.

In addition, students will attend a series of special lectures to be given by distinguished and renowned architects, including the following:

Kenneth Frampton
Architect; professor; author of "Modern Architecture: A Critical History"

Steven Holl
Architect; professor; winner of numerous Progressive Architecture Awards

James Stewart Polshek
Architect; professor; designer for the renovation of Carnegie Hall

Robert A. M. Stern
Architect; professor; author of "Pride of Place"

Bernard Tschumi
Architect; Dean, Columbia University; designer of the park "La Villette", Paris

In the afternoon, the students attend the design studio – an educational method unique to architecture – a place where students are given an intensive training in the skills and critical thinking involved in architectural design. Students, in small groups, work directly with studio instructors to develop their individual designs, which the students then present in periodic reviews or "juries", where they hear the comments and criticism of the invited architects and professors. The design projects given in studio are frequently situated in New York City, so that the student is able to apply the knowledge he or she has gained from the morning sessions. The development of supporting skills such as drawing and model-building is also included in the studio curriculum.

Together the studio and lectures present a comprehensive introduction to every aspect of architecture as it is practiced today. In addition, through the various field-trips and tours, the student learns from the extraordinary examples of architectural and urban design in New York City, the world's preeminent center for architectural culture.

Program Director:
Thomas Hanrahan,
Architect; professor

Introduction to Architecture:
July 6 to August 6
Monday, Tuesday, Wednesday, Thursday
10:00am-5:00pm
3 credits, studio and seminar
Tuition for 1992: $1590
Housing on the Columbia University campus (if required): approximately $600

Applications should include a transcript of the applicant's academic record; a resume summarizing education, employment, and other types of experience; and, where appropriate, examples of the applicant's design work. Also please include a $35 application fee (checks made out to: Columbia University).

Applications are due by June 30

For information and applications write or call:

Office of Admissions -
Introduction to
Architecture Program
Columbia University
Graduate School
of Architecture, Planning
and Preservation
400 Avery Hall
New York, NY 10027
(212) 854 3414

Poster announcing
an introductory course in
architecture.

Purpose
To convey to students the
architectural environment,
and the intensity and excitement of New York City.

Macrostructure
The trapezoidal photograph
of midtown Manhattan
and the yellow circle form
the focal point. The stepped
border, activated by bold
diagonal lines, defines the
background. The black
textblocks and the three
photographs at the bottom
increase the visual depth.

Microaesthetics
The grey trapezoidal plane
unifies the visual elements.
The trapezoidal skewed
grid, referring to the plan
of Manhattan, adds visual
dimension. The soft-focus
edge of the photograph
fuses the image to the
background. The yellow
color of the circle and the
border suggest summer.

18 x 24 in

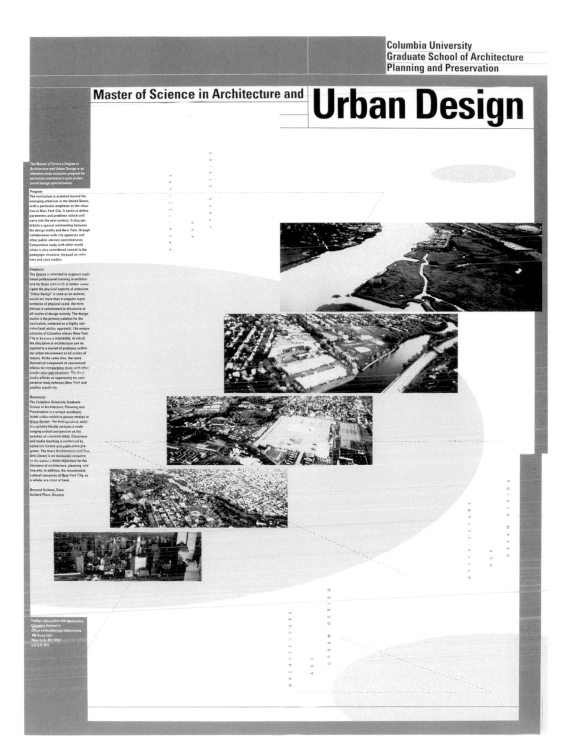

**Columbia University
Graduate School of Architecture
Planning and Preservation**

Master of Science in Architecture and

Urban Design

Poster announcing a program in architecture and urban design.

Purpose
To convey stages of change from the urban environment to the rural landscape.

Macrostructure
The stepped arrangement and increasing size of the five photographs suggest change. The title at the top right completes the stepped composition of the photographs. The active, irregular frame defines the format and anchors the text.

Microaesthetics
The three ovals symbolize the various degrees of urban development, and the three angles allude to possibilities of direction. The small vertical type increases visual depth.

18 x 24 in

Poster announcing
a symposium about
the present and the future
of American cities.

Purpose
To express some of the
issues, present and future,
confronting today's urban
environment.

Macrostructure
The question mark, con-
necting a growing satellite
city and a decaying suburb,
implies the uncertain
future of cities. The torn
edges of the visual field
allude to the erosion
of the urban fabric. The
symposium title placed at
the right hand edge
semantically reinforces
the topic.

Microaesthetics
The photographs' edges
are stepped to represent
progress or torn to convey
decay. The circular
composition of the subtitle
echoes the curves of
the question mark. The
radiating lines signify the
passing of time.

18 x 24 in

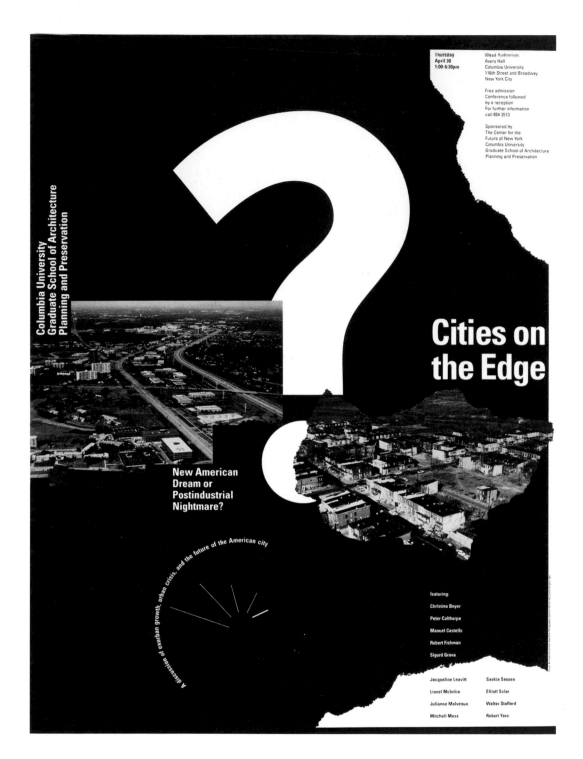

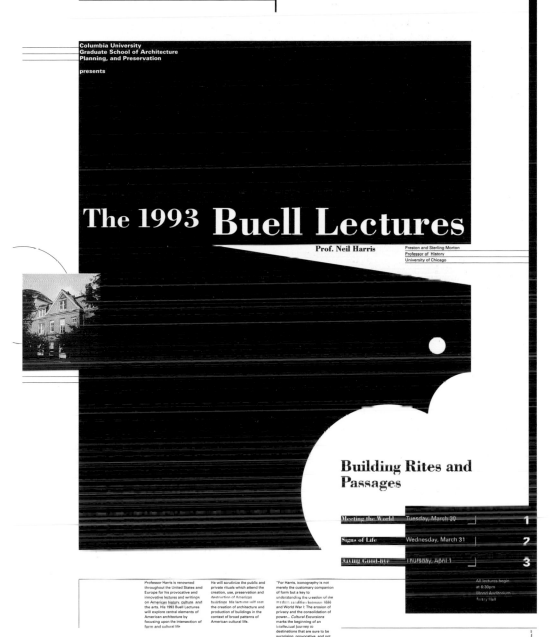

Columbia University
Graduate School of Architecture
Planning, and Preservation

presents

The 1993 Buell Lectures

Prof. Neil Harris

Preston and Sterling Morton
Professor of History
University of Chicago

Building Rites and Passages

Meeting the World	Tuesday, March 30	1
Signs of Life	Wednesday, March 31	2
Saying Good-bye	Thursday, April 1	3

All lectures begin
at 6:30pm
Wood Auditorium
Avery Hall

Professor Harris is renowned
throughout the United States and
Europe for his provocative and
innovative lectures and writings
on American history, culture, and
the arts. His 1993 Buell Lectures
will explore central elements of
American architecture by
focusing upon the intersection of
form and cultural life.

He will scrutinize the public and
private rituals which attend the
creation, use, preservation and
destruction of American
buildings. His lectures will cast
the creation of architecture and
production of buildings in the
context of broad patterns of
American cultural life.

"For Harris, iconography is not
merely the customary companion
of form but a key to
understanding the creation of the
modern condition between 1880
and World War I: The erosion of
privacy and the consolidation of
power... Cultural Excursions
marks the beginning of an
intellectual journey to
destinations that are sure to be
surprising, provocative, and not
yet trampled by hordes of
academic tourists." Karal Ann

18 x 24 in

Poster announcing
a lecture series about the
public and private
rituals associated with
buildings and construction
in America.

Purpose
To express the mystery
and ambiguity of ritual
ceremony, and to under-
score the lectures' role of
illumination.

Macrostructure
The central black field
reflects the mystery embod-
ied in ritual and unifies
the other visual elements.
The cloudlike shape alludes
to popular iconography
and illuminative purpose of
the lectures. The acute
triangle, piercing the black
field, draws attention to
the information about the
speaker. The photograph
establishes a connection
between the central concept
and the lecture building.

Microaesthetics
The title's two type sizes
increase visual depth. The
small white circle acts as a
transitional element bet-
ween the cloudlike shapes
and the acute triangle.

Poster announcing an undergraduate program in architecture, urban planning, and historic preservation.

Purpose
To convey the contrast between the urban fabric of New York and Paris, and to allude to the distance of travel between the two cities.

Macrostructure
The blue triangular field with a wavy edge symbolizes the ocean. The two tapering arcs evoke travel and distance. The juxtaposition of the two schematic maps convey the contrast between New York and Paris.

Microaesthetics
The change from negative to positive invites comparison of the cities through the relations of their names. The negative triangle containing the subtitle connects the school name to the central elements. The text is based on a five-column grid, which also provides the regulating structure for the title and subtitle.

18 x 24 in

Columbia University
Graduate School of Architecture
Planning and Preservation

The
Shape
of Two
Cities

New York

Paris

A Junior Year Introduction to

Architecture, Urban Planning,

and Historic Preservation

held in New York and Paris

A unique undergraduate curriculum in either architecture or in urban planning/historic preservation introduces these fields to mature, intellectually capable students. A full year's academic credit is offered through a carefully constructed program in history, theory, and studio courses. Students are given the academic preparation to enter high-quality graduate programs in the three disciplines as well as graduate programs in the humanities and social sciences.

New York and Paris are the centers of this two-semester program. During the first semester, students live and study in New York and enjoy the resources of Columbia University and the Graduate School of Architecture, Planning, and Preservation. As part of Columbia University, the School offers athletic, computer, and other student facilities; public lectures; extra-curricular activities; the Center for Preservation Research; the Buell Center for the Study of American Architecture; and Avery Library, the nation's finest architecture and planning research collection. Students spend the second semester in Paris based at the program's studio in the historic 17th century Marais district. Students have the choice of either a fall/spring or summer/fall term. All classes and studios are conducted in English.

These cities provide magnificent architectural, cultural, and educational resources. In New York, these include the Museum of Modern Art, South Street Seaport Museum, Cooper-Hewitt Museum, Municipal Art Society, Landmarks Preservation Commission, and the City Planning Commission. In Paris, there are the Louvre, Centre Georges Pompidou, Atelier Parisien d'Urbanisme, Institute Français d'Architecture, Fondation Le Corbusier, Centre National des Recherches Scientifiques, Arts et Metiers, Ecole des Beaux Arts, and Musee Carnavalet. Tours of the cities and lectures by visiting architects, planners, and preservationists are prominent parts of both semesters.

Who should apply
Students interested in architecture, planning, and historic preservation should apply. Because the program is designed to complement the humanities and social sciences curricula of participating colleges, students who plan to pursue graduate level research work in such areas as urban, art, and architecture history, sociology, and economics are also encouraged to apply, especially to the urban planning/historic preservation option.

Admissions
Previous study in architecture, planning, or preservation is not required. The program is designed for students who have completed their sophomore year at an accredited college or university. Admission is selective and enrollment is limited to thirty-five students. Applicants must have the written support of their home institutions. Students are eligible to apply for guaranteed student loans; in addition, a limited number of partial tuition scholarships are available. Application forms and additional information may be obtained from

Dean of Admissions
Columbia University
Graduate School of Architecture,
Planning, and Preservation
400 Avery Hall
New York, NY 10027
212 854 3510

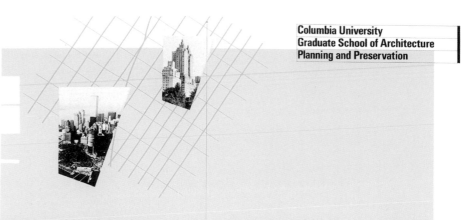

The Shape of Two Cities

New York Paris

A Junior Year Introduction to Architecture, Urban Planning, and Historic Preservation held in New York and Paris

A unique undergraduate curriculum in either architecture or in urban planning/historic preservation introduces these fields to mature, intellectually capable students. A full year's academic credit is offered through a carefully constructed program in history, theory, and studio courses. Students are given the academic preparation to enter high-quality graduate programs in the three disciplines as well as graduate programs in the humanities and social sciences.

New York and Paris are the centers of this two-semester program. During the first semester, students live and study in New York and enjoy the resources of Columbia University and the Graduate School of Architecture, Planning, and Preservation. As part of Columbia University, the School offers athletic, computer, and other student facilities; public lectures, extra-curricular activities; the Center for American Architecture, Avery Library, the nation's finest architecture and planning research collection. Students spend the second semester in Paris based at the program's studio in the historic 17th century Marais district. Students have the choice of either a fall/spring term or summer/fall term. All classes and studios are conducted in English.

These cities provide magnificent architectural, cultural, and educational resources. In New York, these include the Museum of Modern Art, South Street Seaport Museum, Cooper-Hewitt Museum, Municipal Art Society, Landmarks Preservation Commission, and the City Planning Commission. In Paris, there are the Louvre, Centre Beaubourg Pompidou, Atelier Parisien d'Urbanisme, Institut Francais d'Architecture, Fondation Le Corbusier, Centre National des Recherches Scientifiques, Arts et Métiers, Ecole des Beaux Arts and Musée des monuments. Tours of the cities and lectures by visiting architects, planners, and preservationists are prominent parts of both semesters.

Who should apply

Students interested in architecture, planning, and historic preservation should apply. Qualified students in their junior year from participating colleges who plan to pursue graduate level research work in such areas as urban, art, and architecture history, sociology and economics are encouraged to apply, especially to the urban planning/historic preservation option.

Admissions

Previous study in architecture, planning, or preservation is not required. The program is designed for students who have completed their sophomore year at an accredited college or university. Admission is selective and enrollment is limited to thirty-five students. Students who are accepted have the support of their home institutions. Students are eligible to apply for guaranteed student loans. In addition, a limited number of partial tuition scholarships are available. Application forms and additional information may be obtained from:

Dean of Admissions
Columbia University
Graduate School of Architecture,
Planning, and Preservation
400 Avery Hall
New York, NY 10027
(212) 280-3510

18x24 in

Poster announcing an undergraduate program in architecture, urban planning, and historic preservation.

Purpose
To create with some of the elements from the poster on page 144 and four photographs a new solution.

Macrostructure
The grey field unifies all visual components and creates depth. The three different type sizes and the stepped composition of the program title convey distance. The diagonally placed schematic maps and the trapezoidal photographs of New York and Paris invite comparison.

Microaesthetics
The angled subtitle connects the program title and the text. The indent in the title corresponds with the width of the text column. Elements extending outside the grey field and diverging longitudinal and latitudinal lines contribute to the impression of space.

Poster announcing an undergraduate program in architecture, urban planning, and historic preservation.

Purpose
To convey the contrast between New York and Paris and to allude to the physical distance between the two cities.

Macrostructure
The different reading direction of New York and Paris alludes to the two parts of the program and the sequence of the course. The six photographs connect the names of the two cities.

Microaesthetics
The horizontal bars at the top and at the bottom edge reinforce the vertical subdivision of the background space. The width and arrangement of the text and subtitle are based on a six-column grid, which also regulates the macrostructure.

18 x 24 in

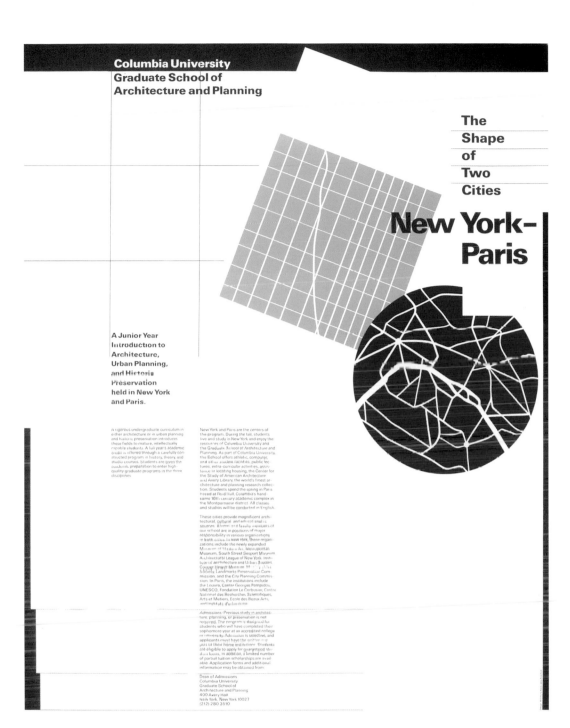

**Columbia University
Graduate School of
Architecture and Planning**

The
Shape
of
Two
Cities

New York–
Paris

A Junior Year
Introduction to
Architecture,
Urban Planning,
and Historic
Preservation
held in New York
and Paris.

A rigorous undergraduate curriculum in
either architecture or in urban planning
and historic preservation introduces
these fields to mature, intellectually
capable students. A full year's academic
credit is offered through a carefully constructed program in history, theory, and
studio courses. Students are given the
academic preparation to enter high-
quality graduate programs in the three
disciplines.

New York and Paris are the centers of
the program. During the fall, students
live and study in New York and enjoy the
resources of Columbia University and
the Graduate School of Architecture and
Planning. As part of Columbia University,
the School offers athletic, computer,
and other student facilities, public lectures, extra-curricular activities, assistance in locating housing, the Center for
the Study of American Architecture
and Avery Library, the world's finest architecture and planning research collection. Students spend the spring in Paris
based at Reid Hall, Columbia's hand-
some 18th-century academic complex in
the Montparnasse district. All classes
and studios will be conducted in English.

These cities provide magnificent architectural, cultural, and educational resources. Alumni and faculty members of
our school are in positions of major
responsibility in various organizations
in both cities. In New York, these organizations include the newly expanded
Museum of Modern Art, Metropolitan
Museum, South Street Seaport Museum,
Architectural League of New York, Institute of Architecture and Urban Studies,
Cooper Hewitt Museum, Municipal Art
Society, Landmarks Preservation Commission, and the City Planning Commission. In Paris, the institutions include
the Louvre, Centre Georges Pompidou,
UNESCO, Fondation Le Corbusier, Centre
National des Recherches Scientifiques,
Arts et Metiers, Ecole des Beaux Arts,
and Institute d'urbanisme.

Admissions: Previous study in architecture, planning, or preservation is not
required. The program is designed for
students who will have completed their
sophomore year at an accredited college
or university. Admission is selective, and
applicants must have the written ap-
proval of their home institutions. Students
are eligible to apply for guaranteed studio loans. In addition, a limited number
of partial tuition scholarships are available. Application forms and additional
information may be obtained from:

Dean of Admissions
Columbia University
Graduate School of
Architecture and Planning
400 Avery Hall
New York, New York 10027
(212) 280 3510

Poster announcing an
undergraduate program
in architecture, urban
planning, and historic
preservation.

Purpose
To convey the basic
contrast between the
urban fabrics of New York
and Paris.

Macrostructure
The square with the grid
of Manhattan and the
overlapping circle with
the map of Paris invite the
cities to be compared.

Microaesthetics
The rectangular cutout
links "Paris" to the circle.
The triangular cutout
anchors the square to
the horizontal band.
Horizontal lines connected
to a series of steps on
the lower left suggest a
multilayer of surfaces.
The line structure at the
top coordinates the typo-
graphic elements.

18 x 24 in

Presented by
Students in the PhD Program
in Urban Planning

TRANSMIGRATION AND SPACE

Conceptualizing the Flows of Globalization

Invited Speakers:

Linda Basch

David Harvey

Terry Plater

Saskia Sassen

Robert Smith

Immanuel Wallerstein

Friday, November 3, 1995
10:00-5:30pm

Columbia University
Avery Hall, Wood Auditorium
116th Street/Broadway
212 854 6280
e-mail: BF45@columbia.edu

Free Admission

Poster announcing
a symposium about the
global shifts of world
population.

Purpose
To express direction
and movement.

Macrostructure
The black field, suggest-
ing a monitor screen,
contains the subtitle and
list of speakers, and
underlines the symposium
title. The rhythmic com-
position of oval shapes in
different sizes implies
movement and depth.

Microaesthetics
The change from negative
to positive of rules and
type facilitates the transition between black field
and white background.
The width of the black field
corresponds with the
two A's left and right in the
title. The typography is
based on a six-column grid
related to the black field.

18 x 24 in

The Origins
of the Avant-garde
in America

1923
1949

The Philip Johnson **February 1, 2, 3**
Colloquium **New York City**

Colomina
Dal Co
Eisenman
Hays
Johnson
Kwinter
Kipnis
Koolhaas
Lavin
Linder
Mertins
Ockman
Rowe
Schwarzer
Singley
Somol

Organized by
the Canadian Centre
for Architecture
in conjunction with
The Museum of
Modern Art, New York
and the
Columbia University
Graduate School of
Architecture, Planning
and Preservation

Session I
Thursday, February 1 Venue: Wood Auditorium, Avery Hall
Columbia University
5:30pm-5:50pm Phyllis Lambert **Introductory Remarks**
5:50pm-7:30pm **Philip Johnson in conversation with Jeffrey Kipnis**

Session II
Friday, February 2 Venue: Wood Auditorium, Avery Hall
Columbia University
9:00am-9:15am Bernard Tschumi **Introductory Remarks**
9:15am-9:30am Robert Somol **Architecture After the Avant-garde**
9:30am-12:15pm **Avant-garde Procedures: Form and Pragmatics**

Francesco Dal Co Victors and Victory: Interpreting Lewis Mumford in the Brown Decades
Detlef Mertins Framing the Constitution: Siegfried Giedion, Emil Kaufmann and the Laws of Architectural Modernity
Joan Ockman The Road Not Taken: Alexander Dorner's Way Beyond Art
Mark Linder An Endless Avant-garde: Frederick Kiesler's Display of Modernism, 1926-1942

Discussion

Session III
Friday, February 2 Venue: Wood Auditorium, Avery Hall
Columbia University
2:00pm-4:45pm **Avant-garde Genealogies: Intimate and Collective Influences**

Michael Hays Mies van der Rohe and the Production of Abstraction
Paulette Singley The Importance of Not Being Earnest
Mitchell Schwarzer The Craft of Art: Henry-Russell Hitchcock and Francesco Dal Co
Sanford Kwinter The Doctrine of Misplaced Concreteness and the American Avant-garde

Discussion

5:00pm-6:30pm **Nostalgia and the Avant-garde by Colin Rowe**

Session IV
Saturday, February 3 Venue: The Roy and Niuta Titus Theater 1
The Museum of Modern Art
9:00am-9:30am Terence Riley **Introductory Remarks**
9:30am-12:30pm **Avant-garde Ideologies**

Silvia Lavin Repressed Memories: Richard Neutra and the Birth Trauma of Modern Architecture
Beatriz Colomina 1949
Rem Koolhaas Le Corbusier, Harrison and the United States
Peter Eisenman The Necessity of an American Avant-garde

Discussion

Admission for all sessions is free on a first-come,
first-served basis. Tickets (free) are required
only for the session at The Museum of Modern Art
and are available at the Lobby Information Desk
beginning January 16.

For information please call:
212 854 3414 (Columbia University) or
212 708 9500 (The Museum of Modern Art)

This colloquium has been undertaken with
the generous support of Peter B. Lewis,
The American Friends of the Canadian Centre
for Architecture, Lily Auchincloss, Mr. and
Mrs. Gustavo Cisneros, Agnes Gund and
Daniel Shapiro, Mr. and Mrs. Ronald S. Lauder,
Marshall S. Cogan, a grant from the
Leo and Julia Forchheimer Foundation, and
Joseph E. Seagram and Sons Ltd.

18 x 24 in

Poster for a colloquium
on the origins of the
avant-garde in America
1923–1949.
Sponsored by the Canadian
Center for Architecture,
The Museum of Modern Art,
and Columbia University.

Purpose
To emphasize the promi-
nence of the speakers
and the time frame of the
symposium topic.

Macrostructure
The vertical band and
the protruding capital letters
emphasize the speakers'
names. The light grey dates
provide a visual transition
from the black type in
the foreground to the white
background.

Microaesthetics
Three vertical white bands
along the right-hand
edge demarcate the three
days of the colloquium.
The two vertical rules act as
transitional elements
between the vertical band
and the field containing
the program information.
The frame around each
session connects the
speakers to parts of the
program.

Two posters announcing
graduate programs in
architecture and
historic preservation.

Purpose
To convey the direction
of each program through
a photograph from
the field of study, and
to develop the typographic
design for each poster
following the particular
image.

Macrostructure
The square photograph,
the large triangular field at
the top reflecting details
from the photograph, and
the vertical name of the
school.

Microaesthetics
The stepped text columns
make reference to the stairs
in the photograph. The
black bar at the bottom left
extends the composition
of the text columns.
The triangle at the bottom
right – contrasting with
the triangle at the top
left – increases the spatial
impression.

**Programs in
Architecture**

**Columbia University
Graduate School of Architecture
and Planning**

**Master of Science in Architecture
and Building Design**
The Master of Science in Architecture and Building Design offers an opportunity to explore specific theories of design, as well as appropriate responses to complex architectural issues.

Master of Architecture
The three-year Master of Architecture program, a first professional degree, develops the skills and provides a basis of judgment necessary for professional work. Studies are centered around the Design Studio, with courses in History, Theory and Technology. In addition, students are encouraged to choose electives which will diversify their curriculum.

The school and its prominent faculty have an excellent international reputation. They are committed to an architecture that solves immediate problems and confronts continuing issues of aesthetic, technical and social importance. To enliven the debate on these issues, many highly-regarded professionals are invited each year to lead a studio or participate in seminars, reviews and lectures.

A one-year Master of Science in Architecture and Building Design and s one-year Master of Science in Architecture and Urban Design are offered as second professional degrees to prospective students who have received a first professional degree in architecture.

**Master of Science in Architecture
and Urban Design**
The focus of the Master of Science in Architecture and Urban Design program is architecture generated in response to an evolving urban context. Its emphasis is on the design of public places.

As part of the Graduate School of Architecture and Planning, these programs are able to draw upon the resources of the master's programs in Historic Preservation, Real Estate Development, and Urban Planning; the Center for Preservation Research; the Buell Center for the Study of American Architecture; and Avery Library, the nation's leading architecture and planning research collection. In addition, there are the resources of the other professional schools of the University, and the countless public and private organizations in New York City.

Faculty members and experienced professional architects and urban designers associated with the school work with the students and assist them in finding employment after they graduate. Scholarships, teaching assistantships, and work-study positions are available. The William Kinne Fellows Memorial Traveling Fellowships provide an opportunity for foreign travel.

Bulletin and application forms may be obtained from:
Dean of Admissions
Graduate School of Architecture and Planning
400 Avery Hall
Columbia University
New York, New York 10027
(212)280.3510

12x24 in

Columbia University Graduate School of Architecture and Planning

Master of Science in Historic Preservation

the nation's oldest historic preservation program provides specialized training for those who wish to be professionally active in preservation as architects, conservators, historians, and planners. The four-year program combines a concern for advocacy with a core of required courses and four concentrations: conservation, design, history and planning. There is also a four-year joint degree program offering qualified students the opportunity to work simultaneously toward master's degrees in architecture and in historic preservation. Any student who has already received a master's degree in architecture may apply for up to twenty-four points of advanced standing toward a master's degree in historic preservation with a design concentration.

As part of the Graduate School of Architecture and Planning, the historic preservation program is able to draw upon the resources of the master's programs in architecture, real estate development, and urban planning; the Center for Preservation Research, the historic preservation program's technical research facility; the Avell Center for the Study of American Architecture; and Avery Library, the nation's leading architecture and planning research collection. In addition, there are the resources of the other professional schools of the University, the Metropolitan Museum of Art, and countless public and private organizations in New York City.

Faculty members and experienced professional preservationists associated with the School work closely with students and assist them in finding pre- and post-graduate employment in public and private agencies in New York City and elsewhere in the nation. Scholarships, teaching assistantships, and work-study positions are available. The William Kinne Fellows Memorial Traveling Fellowships provide an opportunity for foreign travel.

Bulletins and application forms may be obtained from:
Dean of Admissions
Graduate School of Architecture and Planning
400 Avery Hall
Columbia University
New York, New York 10027
(212)280.3510

Macrostructure
The square photograph, the graphic field reflecting details from the photograph, and the vertical name of the school.

Microaesthetics
The undulating edge, the three negative lines, and the two circles echo similar elements in the photograph. The horizontal alignment of the text columns contrasts with the undulating edge of the graphic field. The black horizontal bars at the top and bottom reinforce the vertical space for the type. The three negative lines in the bar at the top reference the baselines of the vertical type.

12 x 24 in

A series of posters announcing lectures and exhibitions at the Columbia University Graduate School of Architecture, Planning, and Preservation.

Purpose

To announce the Fall and Spring semester events, and to explore the wide range of design possibilities with typographic materials. Common throughout the series are the type of information, format, typeface, and vocabulary of typographic elements. The design of the Fall and Spring semester posters of each academic year is based on a similar visual theme.

Macrostructure

The three geometric shapes, referring to the three months of the lecture series, subdivide the list of names. The three sharp triangles point to the exhibition titles protruding from the right.

Microaesthetics

The line structure on the left coordinates the lecture information, day, date, and lecturer's name. The grey vertical band and the parallel line structure stabilize the composition. The intervals between the circles anchoring the seven exhibition titles are determined by an additional structure.

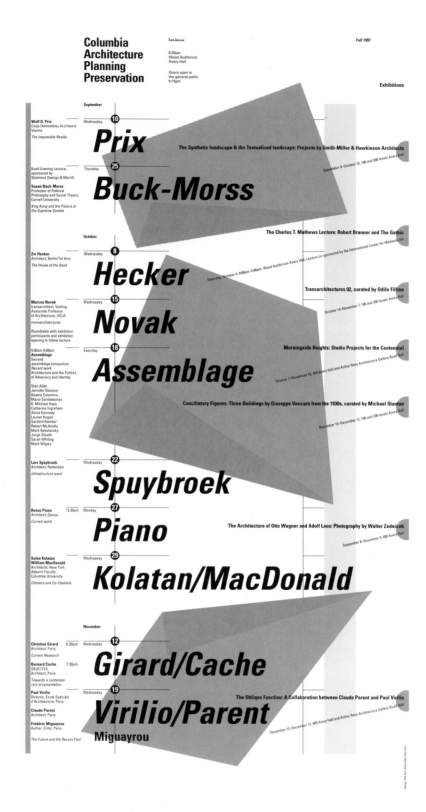

12 x 24 in

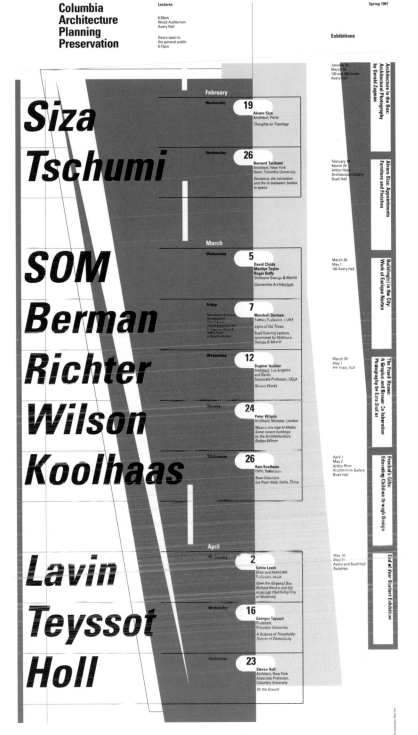

**Columbia
Architecture
Planning
Preservation**

Lectures

6:30pm
Wood Auditorium
Avery Hall

Doors open to
the general public
6:15pm

Spring 1997

Exhibitions

Macrostructure
The lecturers' names are
grouped according to
month. The vertically split
core connects the date,
day, and lecture informa-
tion. The vertical band
bleeding towards the right
carries information
about the six exhibitions.

Microaesthetics
The three line structures
define the space for
information about the
lectures. The white wedge
shape, cutting into the
core from the top left,
intensifies the illusion of
space. The thin vertical
rule on the left emphasizes
the speakers' initials.

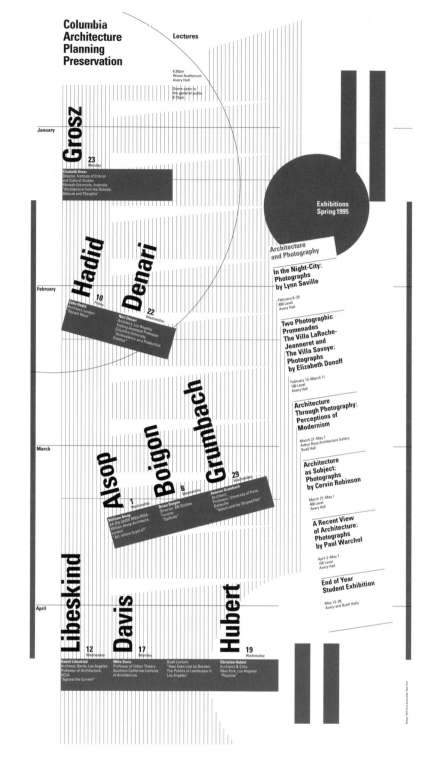

Macrostructure
The four bands with lecture information for each month are freely arranged for visual effect. The circle on the top right and the parallel vertical bands stabilize the angled column of exhibition information.

Microaesthetics
The vertical line pattern, punctuated by ten sharp triangular shapes and a circle, unifies the typographic elements and helps ease the eye's transition to the background.

12 × 24 in

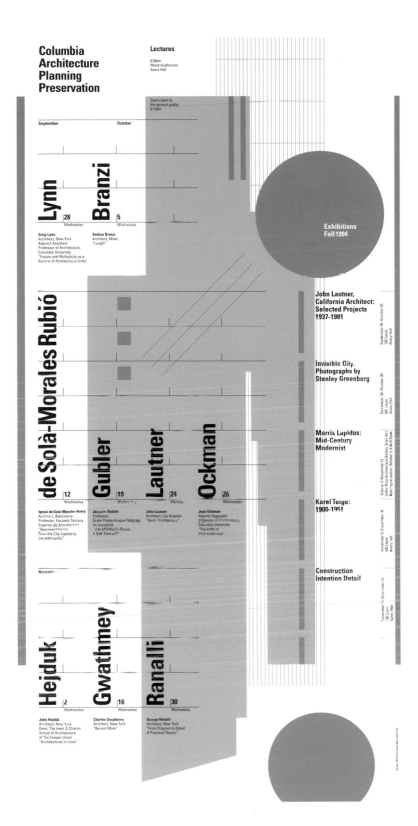

**Columbia
Architecture
Planning
Preservation**

Lectures

6:30pm
Wood Auditorium
Avery Hall

Doors open to
the general public
6:15pm

September   October

Lynn **Branzi**

|28 |5
Wednesday   Wednesday

Greg Lynn
Architect, New York
Adjunct Assistant
Professor of Architecture,
Columbia University
"Fusion and Multiplicity as a
Source of Architectural Unity"

Andrea Branzi
Architect, Milan
"Luoghi"

de Solà-Morales Rubió **Gubler** **Lautner** **Ockman**

|12 |19 |24 |26
Wednesday   Wednesday   Monday   Wednesday

Ignasi de Solà-Morales Rubió
Architect, Barcelona
Professor, Escuela Técnica
Superior de Arquitectura
"Representations:
From the City Capital to
the Metropolis"

Jacques Gubler
Professor,
École Polytechnique Fédérale
du Lausanne
"The Architect's House:
A Self Portrait"

John Lautner
Architect, Los Angeles
"Basic Architecture"

Joan Ockman
Adjunct Associate
Professor of Architecture,
Columbia University
"The Ends of
Postmodernism"

November

Hejduk **Gwathmey** **Ranalli**

|2 |16 |30
Wednesday   Wednesday   Wednesday

John Hejduk
Architect, New York
Dean, The Irwin S. Chanin
School of Architecture
of The Cooper Union
"Architectures in Love"

Charles Gwathmey
Architect, New York
"Recent Work"

George Ranalli
Architect, New York
"From Program to Detail:
A Practical Theory"

**Exhibitions
Fall 1994**

**John Lautner,
California Architect:
Selected Projects
1937-1991**

**Invisible City.
Photographs by
Stanley Greenberg**

**Morris Lapidus:
Mid-Century
Modernist**

**Karel Teige:
1900-1951**

**Construction
Intention Detail**

12 x 24 in

Macrostructure

*The vertical geometric
shape separates the lecture
series on the left from the
exhibitions on the right.
Two circles of different size,
suggesting depth, draw
attention to the exhibitions.*

Microaesthetics

*The line structure on the
left unifies the lecture information, otherwise sepa-
rated into three months.
The subtle pattern of
vertical lines facilitates the
transition from the core
element to the background.
Three diagonal lines
connect the lectures and
exhibition events.*

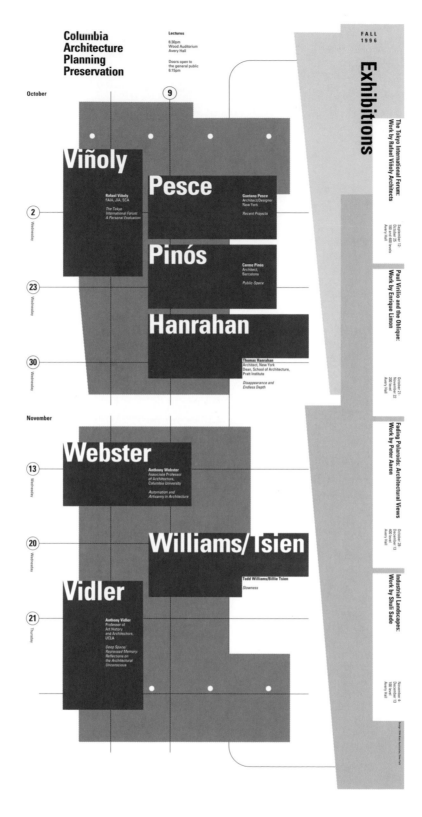

Macrostructure

The seven rectangular shapes carry the lecture information. The two geometric shapes in the background designate the months. The two layered vertical bands on the right contain information about the four exhibitions.

Microaesthetics

The grid structure connects the lecture information with the dates. The four white circles at the top and the three white circles at the bottom refer to the seven lectures and mark the beginning and end of the lecture series.

12 x 24 in

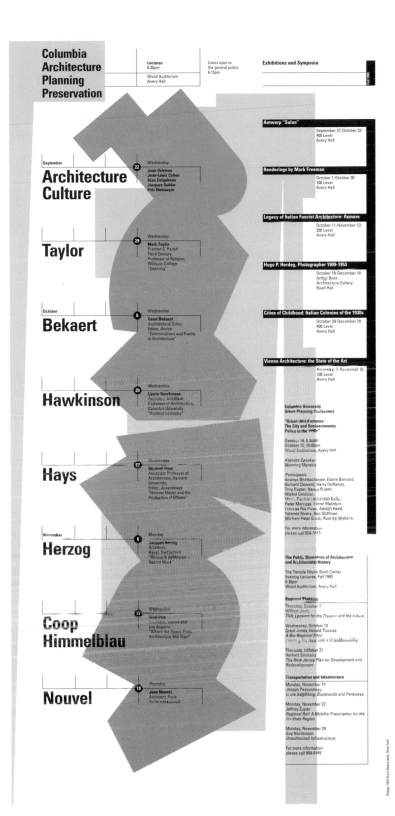

**Columbia
Architecture
Planning
Preservation**

Lectures
6:30pm

Wood Auditorium
Avery Hall

Doors open to
the general public
6:15pm

Exhibitions and Symposia

Fall 1993

September

**Architecture
Culture**

22 Wednesday
Joan Ockman
Jean-Louis Cohen
Alan Colquhoun
Jacques Gubler
Fritz Neumeyer

Taylor

29 Wednesday
Mark Taylor
Preston S. Parish
Third Century
Professor of Religion,
Williams College
"Seeming"

October

Bekaert

6 Wednesday
Geert Bekaert
Architectural Critic;
Editor, Archis
"Commonplace and Poetry
in Architecture"

Hawkinson

20 Wednesday
Laurie Hawkinson
Architect; Assistant
Professor of Architecture,
Columbia University
"Political Economy"

Hays

27 Wednesday
Michael Hays
Associate Professor of
Architecture, Harvard
University;
Editor, Assemblage
"Hannes Meyer and the
Production of Effects"

November

Herzog

8 Monday
Jacques Herzog
Architect,
Basel, Switzerland
"Herzog & deMeuron —
Recent Work"

**Coop
Himmelblau**

11 Wednesday
Wolf Prix
Himmelb/au, Vienna and
Los Angeles
"Where the Space Ends,
Architecture Will Start"

Nouvel

18 Thursday
Jean Nouvel
Architect, Paris
To be announced

Antwerp "Salon"
September 27–October 23
400 Level
Avery Hall

Renderings by Mark Freeman
October 1–October 30
100 Level
Avery Hall

Legacy of Italian Fascist Architecture: Asmara
October 11–November 13
200 Level
Avery Hall

Hugo P. Herdeg, Photographer 1909–1953
October 18–December 10
Arthur Ross
Architecture Gallery
Buell Hall

Cities of Childhood: Italian Colonies of the 1930s
October 29–December 10
400 Level
Avery Hall

Vienna Architecture: the State of the Art
November 7–December 10
100 Level
Avery Hall

**Columbia University
Urban Planning Conference**

"Urban (Mis)fortunes:
The City and Socioeconomic
Policy in the 1990s"

October 14, 6:30pm
October 15, 10:00am
Wood Auditorium, Avery Hall

Keynote Speaker:
Manning Marable

Participants:
Ananya Bhattacharjee, Elaine Bernard,
Richard Cloward, Harry DeRienzo,
Troy Duster, Nancy Fraser,
Michel Gelobter,
Merli, Paulite Fernandez Kelly,
Peter Marcuse, Tinnel McIntyre,
Frances Fox Piven, Adolph Reed,
Yolanda Rivera, Ron Shiffman,
Michael Peter Smith, Rudrick Wallace

For more information
please call 854-3517

**The Public Dimension of Architecture
and Architectural History**

The Temple Hoyne Buell Center
Evening Lectures, Fall 1993
6:30pm
Wood Auditorium, Avery Hall

Regional Planning
Thursday, October 7
William Jordy
TVA: Lessons for the Present and the Future

Wednesday, October 13
Grant James, Ronald Thomas
A Bio-Regional Ethic:
Creating the Next Level of Sustainability

Thursday, October 21
Herbert Simmens
The New Jersey Plan for Development and
Redevelopment

Transportation and Infrastructure
Monday, November 15
Joseph Passonneau
In the Beginning: Boulevards and Parkways

Monday, November 22
Jeffrey Zupan
Regional Rail: A Mobility Prescription for the
Tri-State Region

Monday, November 29
Guy Nordenson
Unauthorized Infrastructure

For more information
please call 854-8165

Design: Willi Kunz Associates, New York

12 x 24 in

Macrostructure
The eight merging geo-
metric shapes refer to the
eight lectures and form
a strong, irregular column
that serves as a core
for structuring typographic
information.

Microaesthetics
Three distinct visual
textures differentiate
lectures, exhibitions, and
symposia. The grey
geometric shape in the
background links the
three disparate compo-
sitions.

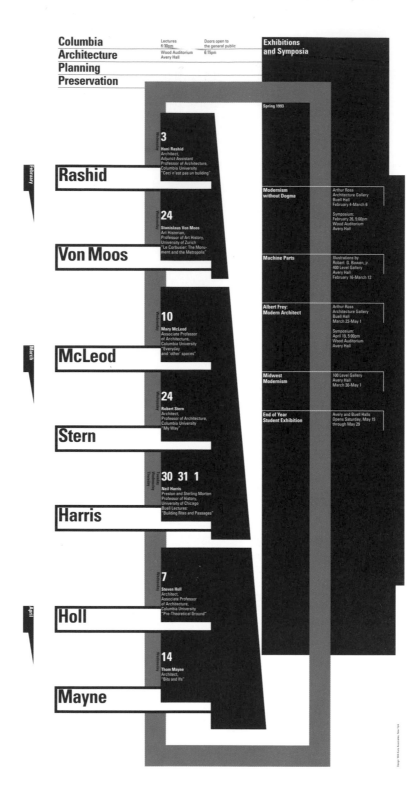

Macrostructure

A central frame links the lecture information on the left and the exhibition listings on the right.

Microaesthetics

The contrast between solid/outline, positive/negative, vertical/slant creates visual depth. The three elements on the left hand edge echo the negative shape between the lecture information and the exhibition listings.

12 x 24 in

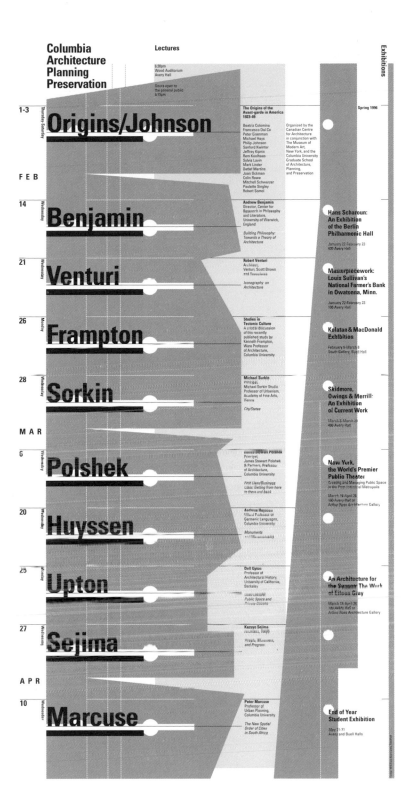

Macrostructure

The geometric shape, punctuated by circles and bold horizontal rules, coordinates the ten lecturers' names with the lecture information. The vertical band, tapered from top to bottom and punctuated with white dots, coordinates the exhibit information.

Microaesthetics

Thin horizontal lines connect the lecture information and the dates. The three sharp triangular shapes, piercing the geometric shape from the right, designate each month. The negative grid of fine lines structures the large geometric shape.

12 × 24 in

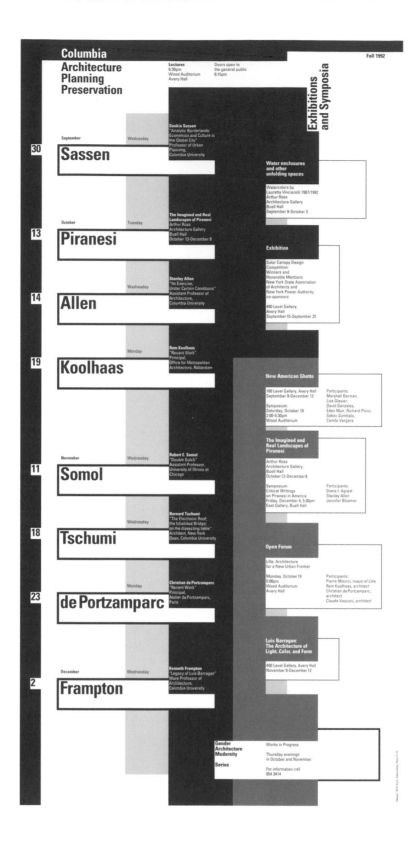

Columbia
Architecture
Planning
Preservation

Lectures
6:30pm
Wood Auditorium
Avery Hall

Doors open to
the general public
6:15pm

Fall 1992

Exhibitions and Symposia

September — Wednesday

30

Sassen

Saskia Sassen
"Analytic Borderlands:
Economics and Culture in
the Global City"
Professor of Urban
Planning,
Columbia University

**Water enclosures
and other
unfolding spaces**

Watercolors by
Lauretta Vinciarelli 1987/1992
Arthur Ross
Architecture Gallery
Buell Hall
September 9–October 3

October — Tuesday

13

Piranesi

The Imagined and Real
Landscapes of Piranesi
Arthur Ross
Architecture Gallery
Buell Hall
October 13–December 8

Exhibition

Solar Canopy Design
Competition:
Winners and
Honorable Mentions
New York State Association
of Architects and
New York Power Authority,
co-sponsors

400 Level Gallery,
Avery Hall
September 10–September 25

Wednesday

14

Allen

Stanley Allen
"Its Exercise,
Under Certain Conditions"
Assistant Professor of
Architecture,
Columbia University

Monday

19

Koolhaas

Rem Koolhaas
"Recent Work"
Principal,
Office for Metropolitan
Architecture, Rotterdam

New American Ghetto

100 Level Gallery, Avery Hall
September 9–December 12

Symposium:
Saturday, October 10
2:00–5:30pm
Wood Auditorium

Participants:
Marshall Berman,
Lisa Glasier,
David Gonzales,
Eden Muir, Richard Plunz,
Sekou Sundiata,
Camilo Vergara

November — Wednesday

11

Somol

Robert E. Somol
"Double Dutch"
Assistant Professor,
University of Illinois at
Chicago

**The Imagined and
Real Landscapes of
Piranesi**

Arthur Ross
Architecture Gallery,
Buell Hall
October 13–December 8

Symposium:
Critical Writings
on Piranesi in America
Friday, December 4, 5:30pm
East Gallery, Buell Hall

Participants:
Diana I. Agrest
Stanley Allen
Jennifer Bloomer

Wednesday

18

Tschumi

Bernard Tschumi
"The Electronic Roof;
the Inhabited Bridge;
on the dissecting table"
Architect, New York
Dean, Columbia University

Open Forum

Lille: Architecture
for a New Urban Frontier

Monday, October 19
5:00pm
Wood Auditorium
Avery Hall

Participants:
Pierre Mauroi, mayor of Lille
Rem Koolhaas, architect
Christian de Portzamparc,
architect
Claude Vasconi, architect

Monday

23

de Portzamparc

Christian de Portzamparc
"Recent Work"
Principal,
Atelier de Portzamparc,
Paris

December — Wednesday

2

Frampton

Kenneth Frampton
"Legacy of Luis Barragan"
Ware Professor of
Architecture,
Columbia University

**Luis Barragan:
The Architecture of
Light, Color, and Form**

400 Level Gallery, Avery Hall
November 9–December 12

**Gender
Architecture
Modernity**

Series

Works in Progress

Thursday evenings
in October and November

For information call
854 3414

Design: Willi Kunz Associates, New York

12 x 24 in

Macrostructure

The vertical core of
a geometric shape links
lecture information
on the left with the
exhibition and symposia
listings on the right.

Microaesthetics

The uniform composition
of the lecture information
on the left contrasts
with the varying size of the
text boxes containing
exhibition and symposia
information on the right.

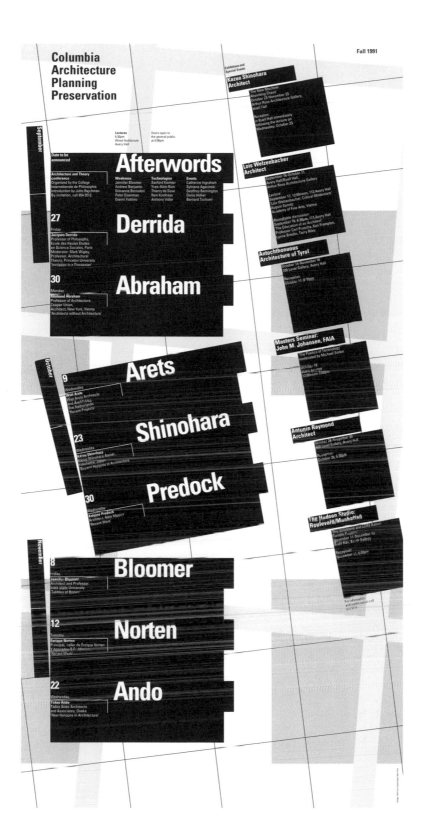

**Columbia
Architecture
Planning
Preservation**

September

Lectures
6:30pm
Wood Auditorium
Avery Hall

Doors open to
the general public
at 6:00pm

Date to be
announced

Afterwords

Architecture and Theory
conference
Organized by the College
Internationale de Philosophie
Introduction by John Rajchman
By invitation, call 854 3512.

Weakness
Jennifer Bloomer
Andrew Benjamin
Giovanna Borradori
Peter Eisenman
Gianni Vattimo

Technologies
Sanford Kwinter
Yves-Alain Bois
Thierry de Duve
Rem Koolhaas
Anthony Vidler

Events
Catherine Ingraham
Sylviane Agacinski
Geoffrey Bennington
Denis Hollier
Bernard Tschumi

27

Friday
Jacques Derrida
Professor of Philosophy,
Ecole des Hautes Etudes
en Science Sociales, Paris
Moderator: Mark Wigley,
Professor, Architectural
Theory, Princeton University
'Invitation to a Discussion'

Derrida

30

Monday
Raimund Abraham
Professor of Architecture,
Cooper Union
Architect, New York, Vienna
'Architects without Architecture'

Abraham

October

Arets

9

Wednesday
Wiel Arets
Wiel Arets Architects
and Associates,
The Netherlands
'Recent Projects'

Shinohara

23

Wednesday
Kazuo Shinohara
Kazuo Shinohara Atelier,
Yokohama, Japan
'Beyond Horizons in Architecture'

Predock

30

Wednesday
Antoine Predock
Architect, New Mexico
'Recent Work'

November

Bloomer

8

Friday
Jennifer Bloomer
Architect and Professor,
Iowa State University
'Tabbles of Bower'

Norten

12

Tuesday
Enrique Norten
Principal, Taller de Enrique Norten
T Arquitectos S.A., Mexico
'Recent Work'

Ando

22

Wednesday
Tadao Ando
Tadao Ando Architects
and Associates, Osaka
'New Horizons in Architecture'

Exhibitions and
Special Events
**Kazuo Shinohara
Architect**

The New Machine:
Absorbing Chaos
October 23-November 23
Arthur Ross Architecture Gallery,
Buell Hall

Reception:
in Buell Hall immediately
following the lecture on
Wednesday, October 23

**Lois Welzenbacher
Architect**

September 18-October 11
Avery Hall/Buell Hall,
Arthur Ross Architecture Gallery

Lecture:
September 17, 12:00 noon, 113 Avery Hall
Lois Welzenbacher: Critical Modernism'
August Sarnitz
Academy of Fine Arts, Vienna

Roundtable discussion:
September 18, 6:30pm, 113 Avery Hall
'The Education of an Architect'
Professor Carl Pruscha, Ken Frampton,
Lynne Breslin, Terry Riley

**Antochthonous
Architecture of Tyrol**

October 14-November 18
100 Level Gallery, Avery Hall

Reception:
October 11, 6:00pm

**Masters Seminar:
John M. Johansen, FAIA**

The Poetics of Technology
moderated by Michael Sorkin

October 16
Public lecture
12:00 noon-2:00pm

**Antonin Raymond
Architect**

October 26-November 30
100 Level Gallery, Avery Hall

Reception:
October 26, 6:30pm

**The Hudson Studio:
Boulevard/Manhattan**

Amy Strickland and Lewis Eaton

November 11-December 13
Buell Hall, Room Gallery

Reception:
November 11, 6:30pm

For information
and continuation call
854 3414.

Macrostructure
The three squares contain information about the three-month lecture series. A slanted column consisting of six squares and rectangles contains the exhibition listings.

Microaesthetics
The two skewed square grids, contrasting in size and weight, further destabilize the visually loose macrostructure. The four grey rectangles in the background add visual depth.

Columbia
Architecture
Planning
Preservation

Exhibitions

1932: A Retrospective
The International Style:
Exhibition 15 and MoMA

Arthur Ross Architecture Gallery
Buell Hall
Opens Monday, March 9
through May 2

	Lectures 6:30pm Wood Auditorium Avery Hall	Doors open to the general public 6:15pm

February

21 Fri — **Mark Wigley**
Assistant Professor,
Architecture,
Princeton University
'Heidegger's House; The
Violence of the Domestic'

Wigley

26 Wed — **Wes Jones**
Holt, Hinshaw,
Pfau & Jones Architects,
Visiting Professor,
Columbia University
'Words, Buildings,
Machines N'

Jones

March

4 Wed — **Anthony Ames**
Principal, Anthony Ames
Architects & Associates,
Atlanta, Georgia
'The Song Remains
the Same'

Ames

9 Mon — **The International Style:**
Exhibition 15 and The
Museum of Modern Art
Arthur Ross
Architecture Gallery
Buell Hall
March 9 - May 2

1932: MoMA

25 Wed — **Kisho Kurokawa**
Architect, Kisho Kurokawa
Architect & Associates,
Tokyo, Japan
'Recent Work'

Kurokawa

April

3 Fri — **Josef Kleihues**
Professor, University of
Dortmund, and
Cooper Union School of
Architecture
Architect, Berlin, Germany
'Poesia Quia Regulae'

Kleihues

6 Mon — **Jean Baudrillard**
Writer, Critic,
Paris, France
'To be announced'

Baudrillard

22 Wed — **Zaha Hadid**
Architect,
London, England
'Recent Work'

Hadid

Tech Talks
Wood Auditorium
6:30pm

Mon, February 17

Anthony Webster
Assistant
Professor
of Structures,
Columbia
University,
'Santiago
Calatrava's Civic
Engineering
Works'

Mon, March 2

James Carpenter
James Carpenter
Associates
'Structure and
Light'

Mon, April 13

Norman Kurtz
Flack and Kurtz
'Intelligent
Buildings and
Environmental
Control
Technology'

Klaus Herdeg:
Formal Structure in
Islamic Architecture
Avery 100
Opens Friday, February 7
6:30pm; through March 14

The Work of Eva Eisler
Avery 400
Opens Monday, February 24
6:30pm; through March 27

Kisho Kurokawa: From
Metabolism to Symbiosis
Avery 100
Opens Wednesday, March 25
through April 18

Autochthonous
Architecture in Tyrol
Avery 400
Opens Monday, March 30
6:30pm; through May 2

Work from Columbia
College and Barnard
Avery 100
Opens Monday, April 20
through April 25

End of Year
Student Exhibition
Avery and Buell Halls
Opens Wednesday, May 6
through May 30

Design: Willi Kunz Associates, New York

12 x 24 in

Macrostructure

*The vertical rectangle,
containing the lecturers'
names and symposium
title, separates the lecture
information on the left
from the exhibition and
tech talks information on
the right. The horizontal
bars containing the
exhibition titles on the right
contrast with the vertical
rectangle.*

Microaesthetics

*The three vertical bands
with different textures
differentiate the tech talks.
The line structures at the
top and at the bottom
increase the illusion of
space. The four horizontal
bands, shifted from the
vertical rectangle, mark the
three months.*

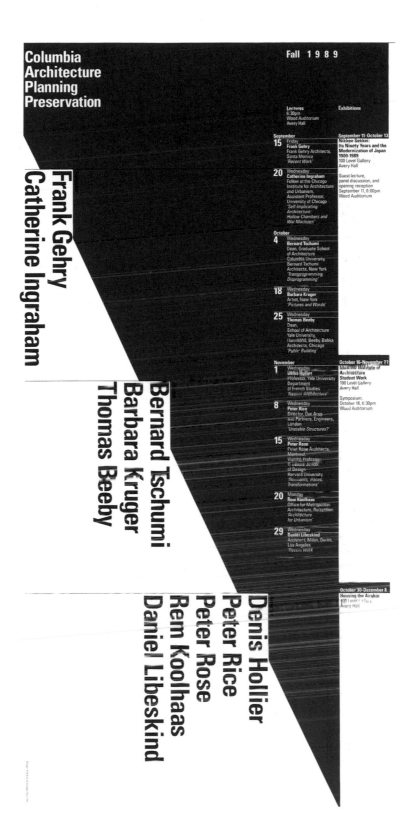

Columbia Architecture Planning Preservation

Fall 1 9 8 9

Lectures
6:30pm
Wood Auditorium
Avery Hall

Exhibitions

September
15 Friday
Frank Gehry
Frank Gehry Architects,
Santa Monica
'Recent Work'

September 11–October 13
Nikken Sekkei:
Its Ninety Years and the
Modernization of Japan
1900-1989
100 Level Gallery
Avery Hall

20 Wednesday
Catherine Ingraham
Fellow at the Chicago
Institute for Architecture
and Urbanism,
Assistant Professor,
University of Chicago
'Self-Implicating
Architecture:
Hollow Chambers and
War Machines'

Guest lecture,
panel discussion, and
opening reception
September 11, 6:00pm
Wood Auditorium

October
4 Wednesday
Bernard Tschumi
Dean, Graduate School
of Architecture
Columbia University,
Bernard Tschumi
Architects, New York
'Transprogramming,
Disprogramming'

18 Wednesday
Barbara Kruger
Artist, New York
'Pictures and Words'

25 Wednesday
Thomas Beeby
Dean,
School of Architecture
Yale University,
Hammond, Beeby, Babka
Architects, Chicago
'Public Building'

November
1 Wednesday
Denis Hollier
Professor, Yale University
Department
of French Studies
'Against Architecture'

October 16–November 22
Moscow Institute of
Architecture
Student Work
100 Level Gallery
Avery Hall

Symposium:
October 18, 6:30pm
Wood Auditorium

8 Wednesday
Peter Rice
Director, Ove Arup
and Partners, Engineers,
London
'Unstable Structures?'

15 Wednesday
Peter Rose
Peter Rose Architects,
Montreal,
Visiting Professor
at Graduate School
of Design
Harvard University
'Remnants, Traces,
Transformations'

20 Monday
Rem Koolhaas
Office for Metropolitan
Architecture, Rotterdam
'Architecture
for Urbanism'

29 Wednesday
Daniel Libeskind
Architect, Milan, Berlin,
Los Angeles
'Recent Work'

October 30–December 8
Housing the Airship
100 Level Gallery
Avery Hall

Frank Gehry
Catherine Ingraham

Bernard Tschumi
Barbara Kruger
Thomas Beeby

Denis Hollier
Peter Rice
Peter Rose
Rem Koolhaas
Daniel Libeskind

Macrostructure
The triangular field con-
nects the lecturers' names
on the left and the lecture
information and exhibition
listings on the right. The
2:3:5 grouping of lecturers'
names is determined by
the three months.

Microaesthetics
The fine texture of the
lecture information con-
trasts with the heavy
vertical band of the exhibit
information.

**Columbia University
Graduate School of Architecture
Planning and Preservation**

Lectures

Exhibitions

Wednesday
Lecture Series
6.30pm
Wood Auditorium
Avery Hall

Gallery
100 Level
Avery Hall

February

4

Trent Schroyer

Professor of Sociology,
Ramapo College, New Jersey

'Political Ecology
of Sustainable Communities'

January 26 - February 20

**'Formal Structure in
Islamic Architecture of
Iran and Turkistan'**

Introductory Talk:
Klaus Herdeg
January 28, 6.30pm
Gallery

11

Allan Temko

Architecture Critic,
San Francisco Chronicle

'Post-Modern Planning
in San Francisco:
A Critical View'

18

Malcolm Quantrill

Architect, Historian,
Critic; Distinguished
Professor of Architecture,
Texas A&M University

'Lateral-Mindedness
versus Literal-Mindedness in
Aalto's Design Thinking'

25

Lin Utzon

Artist

'Works within the Context
of Architecture and
Manufacturing Capacities'

March

4

José Oubrerie

Architect; Associate
Professor of Architecture,
Columbia University

'About Architecture'

February 23 - March 27

**'The Architecture of
Alvaro Siza'**

Introductory Talk:
Kenneth Frampton
February 23, 6.30pm
Wood Auditorium

25

Rainer Crone

Associate Professor
of Art History, Columbia
University; Director,
International Associates
for Contemporary Art

'Kasimir Malevitch and
the Critique of "Objectivity":
"Let wedges cut into
the bosom of space"'

April

1

Jean-Louis Cohen

Professor, Département
de la Recherche,
Ecole d'Architecture,
Paris-Villemin

The Temple Hoyne Buell Lecture

'The American Sources of
Architecture and Urban Form
in Stalinist Russia'

March 30 - April 24

**'The Architecture of
Hiromi Fujii'**

Introductory Talk:
John Whiteman
March 30, 6.30pm
Wood Auditorium

Lecture:
Hiromi Fujii
April 22, 6.30pm
Wood Auditorium

8

Zaha Hadid

Architect; Visiting
Associate Professor
of Architecture,
Columbia University

'Recent Work'

15

Herman Hertzberger

Architect

'Recent Projects:
An Attempt to Make Archi-
tecture as Clothes, ...
Not Just for the Emperor'

22

Hiromi Fujii

Architect, Professor
of Architecture, Shibaura
Institute of Technology

'Works'

Design: Willi Kunz Associates, New York

Macrostructure

*The vertical band coordi-
nates the lecture dates
with the lecturers' names.
The four horizontal bars
on the right structure the
exhibition information.
The circular illustrations
contrast with the
orthogonal overall design.*

Microaesthetics

*The vertical lines along
the bottom edge mark the
horizontal subdivision
of space. The grid structure
coordinates the different
parts of the lecture information. The vertical type
at the top left contrasts with
the horizontally set names
in the lecture calendar.*

12 x 24 in

Columbia University
Graduate School of Architecture
and Planning

SPRING 1986

Lectures and Exhibitions

Jan

Wednesdays
6.00 PM
Wood Auditorium
Avery Hall

29 Robert Campbell
Architect and
Architectural Critic
for the Boston Globe
'Untitled'

Feb

5 Yona Friedman
Architect
Paris, France
'Some New Tasks
for Architects'

12 Elizabeth Plater-Zyberk
Architect and Professor
Andres Duany and
Elizabeth Plater-Zyberk Architects
Coconut Grove, Florida
'Our Work'

Exhibitions
100 Level, Avery Hall

19 Takefumi Aida
Architect
Tokyo, Japan
'My Works and Playfulness
in Japan'

17 Transformed Houses
Lecture by
David Helle
Kenneth T. Jackson
Camilo J. Vergara

26 Mary McLeod
Associate Professor
of Architecture
Columbia University
'To be announced'

Mar

5 Darrell William Westfall
Professor of Architectural History
Chairman, Division of Architectural
History, University of Virginia
'The Forum of Trajan
as Urban Building Block'

Thursdays
6.00 PM
Wood Auditorium
Avery Hall

'The Aesthetics of Technology'

Mario G. Salvadori
Professor Emeritus of Architecture
Columbia University

10 Three Firms

Anthony Ames, Architect
Ralph Lerner Architect
Mayers & Schiff
Associates

19 Lynda Simmons
President, Phipps Houses
New York
'City Survival'

20 Art and Technology
in the Evolution of Cultures

26 Gae Aulenti
Architect
Milan, Italy
'To be announced'

27 The Interdependence
of Art and Technology

Apr

2 Stanley Saitowitz
Architect and
Professor of Architecture
University of California,
Berkeley
'Residential Architecture'

3 High versus
Popular Culture

9 Francesco Dal Co
Architectural Historian
Istituto Universitario
di Architettura di Venezia
The Ruggard Henry Bush Lecture
'On Mies van der Rohe'

10 The Structural Message
of Architecture

12 × 24 in

Design: Willi Kunz Associates, New York

Macrostructure
The bold horizontal rules
subdivide the format
into four bands containing
the information about
lectures and exhibitions.

Microaesthetics
The three vertical bands
differentiate the information
about the two lecture
series and the exhibitions.
The four negative bands
at the top left refer to the
four months lecture
cycle. The fine horizontal
rules subdivide each month
into four weeks.

ROME

Poster for an exhibition
of photographs based on
the city of Rome.

Purpose
To reinforce photographic
content with typography.
The photograph of Roman
ruins in Ostia Antica near
Rome was chosen for its
structure and diversity of
architectural elements.

Macrostructure
The centrally placed photograph determines the
selection, size and placement of the typographic
elements, which echo
the columns, recesses, and
curve of the amphitheater.

Microaesthetics
The title ROME continues
the diagonal movement
of the typographic elements
starting at the bottom left.
The asymmetric typography
contrasts with the visual
composition of graphic
elements. The bold initials
FC draw attention to the
photographer's name. The
square composition of
the exhibition date relates
to the square forms of the
visual elements.

Photographs by
Fredrich **C**antor

July 10   Sheldon Memorial Art Gallery
August 5   University of Nebraska
1979   Lincoln, Nebraska

18 x 24 in

PARIS

Photographs by Fredrich Cantor

Marcuse Pfeifer
Gallery

825 Madison Avenue
New York

Poster for an exhibition
of photographs based on
the city of Paris

Purpose
To reinforce photographic
content with typography.
The photograph of the
Jardin de Luxembourg was
chosen for its rich forms and
interesting composition.

Macrostructure
The centrally placed photograph determines the
selection and placement of
the typographic elements.
The italic title PARIS relates
to the slant of the tree. The
wavy shape at the bottom
left leads from the title to the
exhibition information.

Microaesthetics
The four vertical lines
continue the rhythm of the
fence posts. The detached
i-dot echoes the sitting
figure and its relationship to
the tree's shadow. The
texture of the wavy shape
on the bottom left alludes
to the sand in the photo-
graph. The angled line
adds further visual depth
to the photograph.

18 x 24 in

Index

Recommended reading

A Aicher, Otl
Typography
Berlin: Ernst & Sohn Verlag
1988

B Bosshard, Hans Rudolf
Technische Grundlagen zur
Satzherstellung
Sulgen, Switzerland: Verlag Niggli AG
1980

Bosshard, Hans Rudolf
Typografie Schrift Lesbarkeit
Sulgen, Switzerland: Verlag Niggli AG
1996

Bringhurst, Robert
The elements of typographic style
Vancouver BC: Hartley & Marks
1991

D Dowding, Geoffrey
Finer points in the spacing and
arrangement of type
Vancouver BC: Hartley & Marks
1995

G Gerstner, Karl
Designing programs
Teufen, Switzerland: Arthur Niggli Ltd.
1964

Gerstner, Karl
Compendium for literates
Cambridge MA: MIT Press
1974

Gill, Eric
An essay on typography
Boston: David R. Godine, Publisher
1988

H Hiebert, Kenneth
Graphic design process
New York: Van Nostrand Reinhold
1992

Hochuli, Jost
Das Detail in der Typografie
München: Deutscher Kunstverlag
1990

Hofmann, Armin
Graphic design manual
Sulgen, Switzerland: Verlag Niggli AG
1988

K Kandinsky, Wassily
Punkt und Linie zu Fläche
Bern, Switzerland: Benteli Verlag
1959

Kepes, Gyorgy
Language of vision
Chicago: Paul Theobald
1944

Kinross, Robin
Modern typography
London: Hyphen Press
1992

M McLean, Ruari
The Thames and Hudson
manual of typography
London: Thames and Hudson Ltd.
1980

Meggs, Philip
A history of graphic design
New York: Van Nostrand Reinhold
1992

Moholy-Nagy, László
The new vision
New York: George Wittenborn Inc.
1947

Moholy-Nagy, László
Vision in motion
Chicago: Paul Theobald and Company
1969

Morison, Stanley
First principles of typography
New York: The Macmillan Company
1936

Müller-Brockmann, Josef
Grid systems
Sulgen, Switzerland: Verlag Niggli AG
1988

R Rand, Paul
Thoughts on design
New York: Van Nostrand Reinhold
1970

Rand, Paul
A designer's art
New Haven: Yale University Press
1985

Rand, Paul
Design, form and chaos
New Haven: Yale University Press
1993

Ruder, Emil
Typography
Sulgen, Switzerland: Verlag Niggli AG
1988

S Spencer, Herbert
Pioneers of modern typography
New York: Hastings House Publishers
1970

T Tschichold, Jan
Asymmetric typography
New York: Reinhold Publishing
1967

Tschichold, Jan
The new typography
Berkley: University of California Press
1995

Tschichold, Jan
The form of the book
Vancouver, BC: Hartley & Marx
1991

W Wichmann, Hans
Armin Hofmann:
His work, quest and philosophy
Basel, Switzerland: Birkhäuser Verlag
1989

Wittgenstein, Ludwig
Tractatus logico-philosophicus
London: Routledge
1981

Z Zwimpfer, Moritz
Visual perception
Sulgen, Switzerland: Verlag Niggli AG
1994